Dad

wishing you

enjoyable reading,

Best Wishes

Mike & Kate

x

GREAT BATTLES

GREAT
BATTLES

General Editor: Christer Jorgensen

Bath · New York · Singapore · Hong Kong · Cologne · Delhi · Melbourne

This edition published by Parragon in 2009

Parragon
Queen Street House
4 Queen Street
Bath BA1 1HE, UK

ISBN: 978-1-4075-7485-1

Editorial and design by
Amber Books Ltd
Bradley's Close
74–77 White Lion Street
London N1 9PF
United Kingdom
www.amberbooks.co.uk

Project Editor: Michael Spilling
Design: Hawes Design
Picture Research: Terry Forshaw
Text: Martin J. Dougherty, Michael E. Haskew,
Christer Jorgensen, Chris Mann, Chris McNab,
Michael Neiberg, and Michael Pavkovic

Printed in Indonesia

PICTURE CREDITS

AKG Images: 20, 58/59, 82/83, 92 (bottom), 112, 172/173
AKG Images/Peter Connolly: 26/27, 36 (top), 42/43, 63 (top)
Ancient Art and Architecture Collection: 38 (bottom), 55
Art Archive: 74/75
Art-Tech/Aerospace: 102 (top), 111 (both), 119, 121, 129 (bottom), 136 (bottom), 151 (bottom),152 (bottom), 166,
168 (top), 178 (bottom), 185 (bottom), 192 (top), 194 (top), 209 (both), 210 (bottom), 219 (both), 224-227 (all), 233 (top),
235 (right), 240 (both), 241 (top left and bottom), 242-243 (all), 248 (centre and bottom)
Art-Tech/MARS: 70 (top), 94 (bottom), 105, 137, 164/165, 217 (bottom), 222/223
Bridgeman Art Library: 30 (bottom), 85 (bottom), 87, 110
Corbis: front cover montage (all), 6, 7 (top), 8/9, 15 (bottom), 18/19, 21(bottom), 31, 50/51, 53 (bottom), 78, 84 (top),
94 (top), 98/99, 102 (bottom), 104 (top), 116/117, 124/125, 126, 134, 145, 148/149, 152 (top), 158 (bottom),
193 (bottom), 238/239, 241 (top right)
Nik Cornish: 214/215
Mary Evans Picture Library: 10/11, 12, 23, 39, 53 (top), 76 (bottom), 95, 132/133, 152 (top)
Getty Images: 22 (top), 28, 34/35, 38 (top), 60, 66/67, 90/91, 108/109, 118 (bottom), 120 (top), 128 (bottom),
161 (bottom), 167 (top right), 174/175, 182/183, 184 (bottom), 202, 203 (bottom), 246/247, 250
Heritage Images: 14 (top), 150 (top), 153, 167 (top left), 193 (top)
Photos 12: 44, 46 (bottom), 100/101, 156/157, 190/191, 194 (bottom), 195 (top)
Popperfoto: 198/199, 208
TopFoto: 232 (bottom)
TRH Pictures: 7 (bottom), 140/141, 144, 200, 206/207, 210 (top), 218
Ukrainian State Archive: 216
U. S. Library of Congress: 177 (bottom), 178 (top), 186 (bottom), 187, 230/231, 232 (top)
U. S. Department of Defense: 249, 251 (both)

CONTENTS

INTRODUCTION

History is more than a simple collection of wars and battles. Yet some battles have altered the course of history and with it the fate of the human race. In this book a number of distinguished military historians have presented in a series of short, crisp chapters some 30 battles that were either decisive or great.

s there a difference between greatness and decisiveness? Indeed there is. A battle can be famous without being decisive, a military landmark or even important. It only needs to have the mark of greatness. To give an example: the battle of Adrianople in 378, although a humiliating defeat for the Roman Empire (just like Cannae half a millennium earlier) the battle changed nothing. Even though the glorious edifice that was the Roman Empire was crumbling, it lingered on in the West for another century while the Eastern (Byzantine) Empire existed for another millennium. The German barbarians may have destroyed an army and slain an emperor, but they had only dented Roman might and glory.

THE SCOTS GREYS' CHARGE into the centre of the French line at Waterloo has gone down in the annals of great cavalry encounters. Waterloo was a great battle that ended Napoleon's chances of re-establishing himself as emperor of France.

GREAT BATTLES, GREAT CONSEQUENCES

Then what constitutes a decisive or great battle? Here one has to make use of speculation, so-called counterfactual history, in order to conjure up a vision of what the world would have looked like should an individual battle have turned out differently – in other words, if the defeated party had won the battle and then been able to exploit the resulting victory.

Had the Athenians lost the sea battle of Salamis the Persians would have been able to conquer Greece. As a collection of tributary states, the Greek nations would probably not have played their respective roles as incubators of western European civilizations. That civilization would have borne an imprint of Persian origins.

In 732 Charles Martel defeated the Arabs and as a consequence Islam was confined to the southwestern corner of the European continent. Had Martel lost the battle then the strongest military feudal state in western Europe – the Kingdom of the Franks – would have been crushed and with it an embryonic Christian European civilization. Europe would have been a larger version of Muslim-dominated Al-Andalus (Spain).

Three hundred years later, the battle of Hastings saw the Anglo-Saxons decisively defeated by Duke William of Normandy, giving birth, after another three hundred years, to an English (Anglo–Norman) national identity. Had Harold prevailed, the course of English history would have been different.

This single, decisive battle altered the course of history and made Anglo-Saxon England more European. Equally, had the Spanish Armada in 1588 swept the sea of Drake and Howard's fleets, combined with Parma's army in Flanders and landed on England's shores, then Britain would have been re-Catholicized. As a consequence, there would probably have been no British empire and the history of the world would have been altered irrevocably.

Two decisive battles from the American Civil War are also featured: Antietam and Gettysburg. Although both battles were technically 'draws', these two epic encounters undermined the Confederacy's ability to wage war and contributed to the Union's victory over the Southern states.

Some of the major battles of the twentieth century are also featured. On the beaches of Normandy, the Allies sought to begin the liberation of Europe from the Nazis on 6 June 1944. The success or failure of the largest seaborne invasion in the history of warfare would define the future of Western Europe.

Yet a battle does not need to be decisive or even important from a military point of view to be a great battle. It simply needs to be great because of its commanders, the use of some new tactic, weaponry or formations or it could – like Constantinople – have a vital symbolic value as the end of one era or the beginning of a new epoch. Greatness, like military glory, is fickle and fleeting and changes with time. But some of it endures down the centuries having become immortal as well as being touched by greatness and that is why we – both writers of great battles and the readers – continue to discuss, read and write about such battles. Great battles endure because they have something more than most military encounters and therefore continue to keep us enthralled down the ages.

The authors of this volume of great battles sincerely hope that you the reader share our fascination for the great military battles of the past.

Christer Jorgensen, General Editor

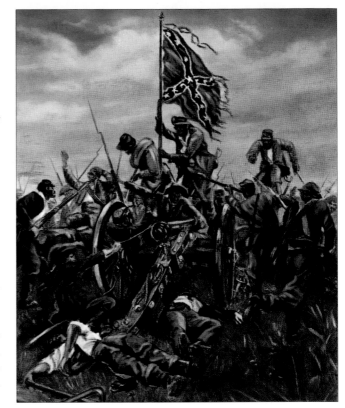

ALTHOUGH ULTIMATELY *achieving very little, the forceful charge of Pickett's Confederate infantry against the Union centre at the battle of Gettysburg in 1863 has gone down in military folklore for its dash and bravery.*

A GERMAN OFFICER *scans the horizon amidst the rubble of Stalingrad, October 1942. The battle of Stalingrad involved some of the most ferocious urban fighting ever seen in the history of warfare. The Soviet destruction of the German Sixth Army decisively turned the war on the Eastern Front.*

THE AGE OF
THE SWORD

The individual warrior dominated much of warfare in the Ancient and Medieval eras, often fighting in massed, ill-disciplined hordes. It was the rise of Sparta in Ancient Greece that showed what a professional, disciplined force of heavily armed infantry could do in the face of superior numbers and this was brought to climactic fruition with Alexander the Great's seemingly-invincible Macedonian phalanxes. Later, the Romans created the most complete, efficient professional army of the Ancient era: their use of well-drilled, tightly packed infantry cohorts dominated the battlefields of Europe and the Mediterranean for centuries.

However, with the demise of the Roman empire, military technology and professionalism regressed – only the Normans and Byzantines kept the tradition of the professional soldier alive. From the fourteenth century onwards, during the High Middle Ages, professional armies again began to dominate the battlefield, and, as seen at Agincourt, such armies could decisively defeat a numerically superior foe.

THIS FIFTEENTH-CENTURY MANUSCRIPT ILLUSTRATION of the capture of Damietta (1219) in Egypt during the Fifth Crusade shows the very bloody and personal nature of hand-to-hand fighting with swords. The sword was the dominant sidearm until the development of arquebus and pistol in the Sixteenth century.

MARATHON 490 BC

At Marathon, an outnumbered force of Greek hoplites seized a chance to defeat their Persian foes, exploiting their superior armour and discipline to win one of the most famous tactical victories of the Ancient World. It was, however, not the end of the Persian threat to the independent Greek city-states.

By 539 BC the Persians under Cyrus the Great had conquered much of Anatolia, including those Greeks living in Ionia on the coast. Initially, relations between the Persians and their Greek subjects were relatively cordial. Over the course of the next several decades a number of tensions emerged which soured that relationship. The Persians impeded the Greeks' economic development with trade restrictions. Moreover, the autocratic Persians imposed puppet tyrants on the Ionian city-states – something antithetical to the independent-minded Greeks. In 499 BC the Ionians finally broke into open revolt against the Persians. Their leader, Aristagoras of Miletus sought aid from the states on the Greek mainland. His first

MARATHON FACTS

Who: Nearly 11,000 Athenians and Plataean hoplites, led on the day of the battle by the Athenian general Militiades, were opposed by a multi-ethnic Persian army numbering perhaps 25,000, under the command of the Persian Artaphernes and the Median noble Datis.

What: The Athenians weakened the centre of their line and strengthened their wings, allowing the Persians to push through the centre, only to be defeated on the flanks and have their centre enveloped by the victorious wings of the Greek army.

Where: The Plain of Marathon, about 41.8km (26 miles) from Athens.

When: 12 August 490 BC.

Why: The Persians wanted to attack Athens to punish the city for its support for the rebellion of the Ionian Greek cities.

Outcome: The Persians were driven from Greece for 10 years.

At the Battle of Marathon Militiades, with 10,000 Athenian and 400 Plataean hoplites, defeated a Persian force nearly double their size, including 10,000 Immortals, proving the value of the phalanx infantry formation.

RELIEF OF IMMORTALS at the Apadana, Persepolis, Iran. The Immortals were an elite royal guard within the Achaemenid Persian army. Only ethnic Persians or Medeans could be members of the unit which, according to the Greek historian Herodotus, always numbered precisely 10,000 men.

could expect Spartan reinforcements and the presence of such tough, well-disciplined hoplites would dramatically transform the military balance on the Plain of Marathon. As a result, the Persians began to embark a part of their forces on the transports so that they could sail for Athens the next morning while the remainder of their forces kept a watch on the Athenian and Plataean hoplites at Marathon. Even without the shield signal, the Persians could hope for help from within the city if the army were away.

This force was to be under the command of Datis and seems to have included the majority of the cavalry who would be very useful in making a dash for Athens once the task force made landfall at Phaleron Bay. Artaphernes would stay at Marathon and maintain a close blockade of the Athenian camp. He probably had about 15,000 men with him, almost exclusively infantry. Fortunately for the

Athenians, they were alerted to the Persian plan by some sympathetic Ionians who were serving with the Persians. They sent the famous message 'the cavalry are away' which galvanized the resolve of the Athenian commanders to offer battle. Indeed, the 10 Athenian strategoi, generals elected from each of Athens' 10 tribal divisions, were deadlocked as to whether or not to stay put and fight, return to Athens, as they, too, were mindful of treachery from within the city, or to offer battle, a course of action favoured by Militiades.

Fortunately, the War Archon (a ceremonial position in which the holder can cast the deciding vote in the case of such a deadlock) supported staying at Marathon and advancing against the Persians. The decision was made to launch an attack at dawn. If they could quickly and decisively defeat Artaphernes' troops it would be possible to make a forced march along the coastal road to Athens and arrive before the Persian assault force.

The next morning saw the opposing forces arrayed for battle. Militiades, who understood Persian tactics, was in command that day, and deployed the Greek forces. He knew that the Persians were likely to put their best troops in the centre of their battle line and that the Persian numbers would make it likely that if he arrayed his phalanx eight-deep along the entire front, they would be outflanked. In order to prevent this he made the centre of his line thinner, knowing that the Persians would initially have success there.

However, Militiades also knew that the wings of the Persian formation would be formed from lighter-armed and less enthusiastic levies and that the heavily-armed wings of the Greek army would be victorious. He therefore ordered that the wings not pursue the defeated levies but once they had been driven off, to wheel inwards on the Persian centre. The right wing was under the command of the War Archon Callimachus and the left was formed by the Plataeans.

Artaphernes deployed his troops as Militiades had expected. His best troops, Iranian soldiers from the standing army and tough Saka mercenaries, formed the centre of his formation with various levies, including unenthusiastic Ionian Greeks, on the flanks. In order to maintain his close

CLASSIC HOPLITE HELMETS, from left to right: a simple Corinthian helmet; the classic Corinthian design with long cheek pieces; a later Illyrian helmet; and a late Corinthian design with a space cut out for the wearer's ears to improve their hearing.

SPARTAN HOPLITES PREPARE FOR BATTLE. Male Spartan children were bred to be warriors from a very young age. They ate sparingly but well, exercised and trained daily. Just as important was the attitude engendered. They, and the rest of Greece, knew they were the best. Confidence in victory gives a man a huge advantage in a fight.

blockade of the Athenian camp, he advanced to within eight stades, or 1.6km (1 mile), of the Greek positions.

The Greeks advanced from their camp towards the Persian lines. Herodotus recounts that they did so at the run, to reduce the considerable number of arrows that would be shot by the Persians, many of who carried bows. This is very unlikely since to run a mile in heavy hoplite armour would have been nearly impossible and unnecessary – the Athenians likely broke into a jog at about 137m (150 yards) – the range of a Persian bow. The battle lines engaged and the Persians had the better of it in the centre where the best of the Persian troops were posted and the Athenians were pushed back. On the wings, however, the levies were routed. Following their orders, the victorious Greeks wheeled in against the Persian centre catching them in a double envelopment. A slaughter followed with 6400 Persian casualties, mostly Iranian and Saka troops, and only 192 Athenians, including Callimachus, and a handful of Plataeans killed. The Greeks also captured seven Persian ships although the others escaped.

AFTERMATH

The Athenians, could not, however, rest after their victory. While one tribal division held the field, the remainder made a forced march back to Athens. They arrived in time to deter the Persians from landing and so Datis, now joined by Artaphernes' survivors, was forced to return home. While the Athenians and Plataeans had won a great victory, they had not really won the war.

The Persians returned home and almost immediately began preparations for another campaign – although it would take 10 years, the Persians would return in force with any eye to conquering all of Greece, not just punishing the Athenians.

POPULAR MYTH HAS IT that following the Greek victory at Marathon, the Athenian runner, Philippedes, delivered the news to the worried Athenians 42km (26 miles) away. The modern marathon race celebrates his feat.

MARATHON

5 Philippides allegedly runs the 42km (26 miles) to Athens to proclaim the news of the Greek victory before dying of fatigue.

2 In the centre, the Persian line counter-attacks and successfully breaks through the Athenian phalanx.

1 The Greek phalanx advances at a run towards the Persians, whose flanks quickly give way under pressure.

3 At the crucial moment, the Greek wings abandon their pursuit and attack the flanks of the Persian centre.

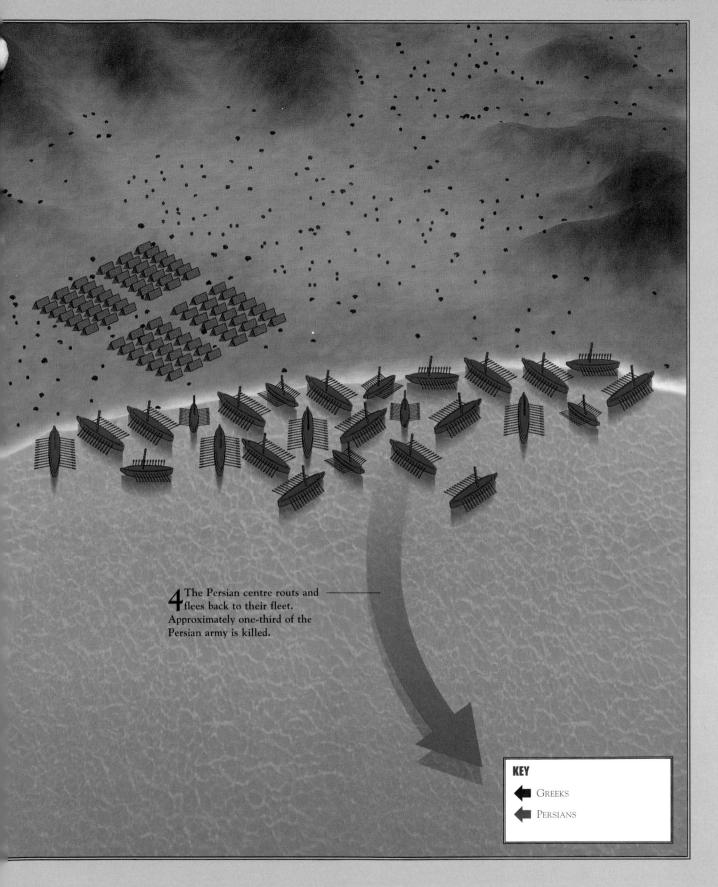

4 The Persian centre routs and flees back to their fleet. Approximately one-third of the Persian army is killed.

KEY

⬅ GREEKS

⬅ PERSIANS

SALAMIS

480 BC

On land and sea, the Persian Great King Xerxes moved with massive force against the Greek city-states, principally Athens and Sparta. At Thermopylae, a mere 300 Spartan hoplites sacrificed themselves to buy precious time. At Salamis, the Greeks inflicted a crushing naval defeat upon the invaders and preserved the flower of Western culture.

During the fifth century BC, the vast empire of Persia was at the height of its glory. The realm of King Darius I extended from the Caucasus to the Indian Ocean and from the shores of the Mediterranean Sea to the Indus River, and his subjects included a great diversity of peoples. Among these were the Ionian Greeks, who had settled on the western coast of Asia Minor. In 500 BC, the Ionians rose in rebellion against Darius. They were defeated after six years of bitter fighting. The people of Athens had recognized their ancestral ties with the Ionians and burned the Persian city of Sardis. In 491 BC, Darius sought to punish the Athenians for their interference in what he considered a domestic affair.

SALAMIS FACTS

Who: A combined Greek naval force under the Athenian Themistocles and numbering 300 triremes opposed 400 Persian triremes commanded by several admirals as Xerxes (d. 486 BC) watched from nearby heights seated on a golden throne.

What: The Persian fleet was routed and fled in confusion after being lured into shallow waters, surrounded and set upon by the rams of the Greek vessels.

Where: In the Saronic Gulf near the island of Salamis, west of modern Athens, Greece.

When: 20 September 480 BC.

Why: The Persian Great King Xerxes intended to avenge the defeat of his father,

Darius, at Marathon a decade earlier and extend his empire into Europe.

Outcome: The Persians suffered grievous losses and were compelled to withdraw. Greek civilization was preserved and continued to flourish.

SEA WARFARE In the Ancient world, as shown here in this nineteenth-century painting of the Battle of Salamis, was a chaotic, messy affair that was often decided by the judicious deployment of forces before the battle.

His punitive expedition, however, met with disaster on the plain of Marathon. Forced to drink the bitter dram of defeat, Darius died after a 36-year reign, his thirst for vengeance unquenched.

ENTER XERXES

When Xerxes, the son of Darius, ascended the throne of Persia, he did not initially embrace his father's quest for revenge. However, after crushing a revolt in Egypt, he called his advisors together to discuss another military move against Athens. 'As you saw, Darius himself was making preparations for war against these men. But death prevented him from carrying out his purpose,' Xerxes thundered. 'I, therefore, on his behalf and for the benefit of all my subjects, will not rest until I have taken Athens and burnt it to the ground. … If we crush the Athenians and their neighbours in the Peloponnese, we shall so extend the empire of Persia that its boundaries will be God's own sky.'

During an average lifetime, a citizen of Athens might have personally known such intellectual giants as Socrates, Aeschylus, Sophocles, Euripides and Aristophanes. The heirs of Western culture in philosophy, medicine, mathematics, drama and democracy owe their existence to such men. Athens and Sparta, the principal Greek city-states, had coexisted though their relations were strained at times. Facing a growing threat from the Persians, it was apparent to the Greeks that cooperation and mutual defence offered their only hope for survival. In 482 BC, a rich vein of silver had been discovered in the mines at Laurium, near Athens. During the heated debate which swirled around the highest and best use for the new-found wealth, the voice of Themistocles was clear and persuasive. Athens must expand her navy to counter the threat of Persian invasion. Themistocles had undoubtedly considered that the Persians would require large numbers of ships to transport the necessities of war if they approached Greece once again. He was also aware of the fighting proficiency of the heavily armed Spartan hoplites on land.

THE CAMPAIGN

The Greek historian Herodotus wrote that the Persian army numbered five million men and that it drank rivers dry as it passed. A more realistic number would be approximately 500,000. The Persian fleet was said to consist of 1207 triremes, so named because the vessels were powered by oarsmen in three rows. Early in the campaign, the Persians accomplished a pair of major engineering feats. They bridged the Hellespont, today known as the Dardanelles, with a pair of spans roughly 1280m (1400 yards) long. When a storm wrecked the first bridges, two replacements were constructed. The Persians also spent three years digging

'THE SEA BATTLE OF SALAMIS' – a romantic depiction of the battle by German artist Wilhelm von Kaulbach (1804–74).

A GREEK BIREME dating from the fifth century BC. It has a prominent ram at its prow. Note the chair provided for the helmsman, who has two large paddles to act as a rudder.

a canal 2.4km (1.5 miles) wide across an isthmus near Mount Athos. Finally, 10 long years after its humiliating defeat at Marathon, the Persian army was again on the move toward Greece. A number of Greek cities pledged allegiance to Xerxes as his juggernaut advanced inexorably toward them. Athens and Sparta, however, remained defiant against overwhelming odds.

THERMOPYLAE

On 18 August, the advancing Persians reached the pass at Thermopylae, through which the force had to move in order to reach Athens. The Persians drew up before the pass, which was barely 15m (50ft) wide and defended by 6000 Spartan hoplites under the command of their king, Leonidas. Time after time, the Persians charged the Spartans, and each time they were repulsed with heavy losses. Even the 'Immortals', the elite of the Persian army and well known for their dash and élan, failed to carry Thermopylae (which translates as 'pass of the hot springs').

Some of the troops with Leonidas departed, and controversy persists as to whether the king dismissed them with contempt or withdrew them to fight another day. Whatever the truth, the end was nearing for the 300 Spartans who remained on the third day of the fight at Thermopylae. A Greek traitor named Ephialtes showed the Persians an alternate route over the mountains, which would allow them to attack the Spartans from the rear. Herodotus wrote that he committed the names of the 300 Spartans who stood their ground to memory 'because they deserved to be remembered'.

When one Spartan was told that the Persians would loose so many arrows that they would darken the sky, he replied, 'This is pleasant news … for if the Persians hide the sun we shall have our battle in the shade.' Killed to the last man, the Spartans claimed the lives of two of Xerxes'

brothers. Years after the battle, a plaque was erected to commemorate the stand of Leonidas and his men. It read: 'Go tell the Spartans, you who read: We took their orders and are dead.' The heroic Spartans of Thermopylae did not sacrifice themselves in vain. Their stand cost the Persians precious time, and a pair of violent storms sank more than 200 Persian ships. Themistocles, meanwhile, had led the Greek fleet to victory at the Gulf of Pagasae and Artemisium. When he received the news that the Persians had taken Thermopylae, Themistocles withdrew his fleet to the island of Salamis, which offered safe harbour.

DELAY AND DECEPTION

By the time the Persian army reached Athens, most of the citizenry had fled. Those who had not were put to the sword. The city, including the Acropolis, was looted and burned. Still, in order to win a decisive victory, Xerxes had to defeat the Greek army on land. To defeat the Greek army, his triremes had to be able to manoeuvre in safety. Therefore, a victory over the Greek fleet became an immediate necessity. As Themistocles had predicted years earlier, the decisive battle in the life of Athens, and indeed all of Greece, would take place at sea.

IT IS SAID THAT PERSIAN KING XERXES I (right) was so confident of victory he had a throne set up on the shore, to watch the battle in style and record the names of commanders who performed particularly well.

THE GREEKS CELEBRATE their victory over the Persian navy in the Battle of Salamis, which took place in the Gulf of Aegina near Athens, September 480 BC. This painting was by nineteenth century artist F. Cormon.

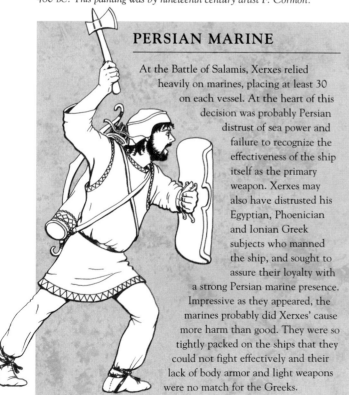

PERSIAN MARINE

At the Battle of Salamis, Xerxes relied heavily on marines, placing at least 30 on each vessel. At the heart of this decision was probably Persian distrust of sea power and failure to recognize the effectiveness of the ship itself as the primary weapon. Xerxes may also have distrusted his Egyptian, Phoenician and Ionian Greek subjects who manned the ship, and sought to assure their loyalty with a strong Persian marine presence. Impressive as they appeared, the marines probably did Xerxes' cause more harm than good. They were so tightly packed on the ships that they could not fight effectively and their lack of body armor and light weapons were no match for the Greeks.

As Xerxes neared the narrow isthmus which connects northern Greece with the Peloponnese, the Spartans and other Peloponnesians built a wall and other defensive positions. Themistocles then demonstrated his true military genius by sending a slave named Sicinnus to Xerxes with false information. Sicinnus gave Xerxes a report of dissent among the allied Greeks and noted that the morale of the Greek forces was waning. In fact, he said, the Greek commander himself was sympathetic to Xerxes and wished for a resounding Persian victory. Preventing the escape of the disorganized Greeks would ensure a triumph. Xerxes took the bait and weakened his force by sending a squadron of Egyptian vessels to cover potential escape routes.

DISPOSITIONS

Xerxes planned simply to overwhelm the 300 Greek triremes which opposed his force of 400 vessels in the narrow waters around Salamis. Themistocles, however, had other ideas. He deployed his fleet with the Athenians and Corinthians on the left, the Aegenitans and Spartans on the right, hoping that the Persians would be drawn into the shallow and narrow waters near the Bay of Eleusis. As the Persians approached, most of the Greek triremes would be obscured from their view by a nearby island. In order to lure the Persians to their doom, Themistocles would order the 50 Corinthian triremes under his command to hoist their sails and feign retreat.

A PERSIAN ADMIRAL, the bravest of the brothers of King Xerxes, is killed by the Greeks at the Battle of Salamis (by William Rainey, from an illustrated history of Plutarch's Lives).

The Persian triremes, apparently constructed for combat on the open sea, would find manoeuvring virtually impossible in the narrows. They were heavier than those of the Greeks and sat higher in the water while carrying up to 30 infantrymen or archers as opposed to 14 aboard the Greek vessels.

THE BATTLE

On the morning of 20 September 480 BC, Xerxes ascended a golden throne on the heights above Salamis. The Greek oarsmen were reported to have sung a hymn to the god Apollo as they struck the Persian vanguard, overextended in its pursuit of the supposedly retreating Corinthians. When the commanders of the leading Persian ships realized that they had fallen into a trap, they ordered a backwater. However, those vessels behind them had nowhere to go, throwing the fleet into confusion. The Persians' superior numbers had now become a hindrance rather than an advantage.

A line of Greek triremes moved in orderly fashion to encircle the confused enemy, and their bronze rams inflicted deadly punishment on the foundering Persian ships. Aeschylus, who is remembered as the father of literary tragedy, fought at both Marathon and Salamis. He described the scene as reminiscent of the mass netting and killing of fish on the shores of the Mediterranean. 'At first the torrent of the Persians' fleet bore up,' Aeschylus wrote. 'But then with the press of the shipping hemmed there in the narrows, none could help another.'

Standing off from the tangle of Persian with Persian, the Greeks struck virtually at will. Aeschylus related a grisly scene as if from the Persian perspective. 'The hulls of our vessels rolled over and the sea was hidden from our sight, choked with wrecks and slaughtered men. The shores and reefs were strewn with corpses. In wild disorder every ship remaining in our fleet turned tail and fled. But the Greeks pursued us, and with oars or broken fragments of wreckage struck the survivors' heads as though they were tunneys and a haul of fish. Shrieks and groans rang across the water until nightfall hid us from them.'

AFTERMATH

The Persian fleet was crippled at Salamis, losing 200 triremes, roughly half its strength, to a mere 40 for the Greeks. In the wake of the disaster, Xerxes had little choice but to retire to safety, lest the Greeks sail northward and destroy the bridges over the Hellespont, severing his overland supply route.

The Greeks did not immediately recognize the magnitude of their victory. There was still some fighting to be done. When Xerxes departed, he left a force of 300,000 soldiers under the command of Mardonius. The following spring, the Persians captured Athens once again, but that summer the combined armies of the Athenians and Spartans forced Mardonius northward, defeating him decisively at Plataea in September. During the same month, a Greek fleet commanded by Xanthippus defeated the Persians once again at Mycale.

Greece was at last free from the threat of Eastern domination. For half a century Athens maintained the strongest fleet in the Ancient World, while the army of Sparta was the preeminent force on land. Increasing rivalry and distrust eventually brought the two city-states to war with one another. Ironically, the names of Marathon, Thermopylae and Salamis were remembered with reverence by both. It had been a time when Greek stood with Greek and these victories had shaped the course of human history.

SALAMIS

4 The Greeks suddenly turn and launch themselves at the Persians who are thrown into confusion.

5 Xerxes watches in rage as his fleet is defeated in the narrow strait.

1 The Corinthians and other Greeks hurriedly make sail in a seeming attempt to flee from the Persian ships.

2 The Persian fleet follows the 'fleeing' Greeks into the narrow strait, where their ships cannot manoeuvre easily.

3 The Greek right wing, previously hidden from sight, attack the Persian fleet in the flank, taking them by surprise.

KEY

GREEK NAVY

PERSIAN NAVY

GAUGAMELA 331 BC

Gaugamela was one of Alexander's greatest triumphs. Outnumbered five to one, the Macedonians outfought their Persian foes as Alexander out-generalled Darius, despite the Great King fighting on ground of his own choosing, specially prepared for special weapons such as scythed chariots and war elephants.

Alexander inherited more than a kingdom from his father, Philip II of Macedon. He inherited a powerful military instrument and the desire to use it. Philip had fought for many years to unify the kingdom of Macedon and impose his power over neighbouring Greeks and barbarians. The army he forged to do it was the basis for Alexander's conquests. Had Philip not been assassinated at the age of 46, he and not Alexander might have made war upon great Persia.

Alexander was raised as a Greek prince should be, on heroic tales from the epic poetry of Homer. He was part of a culture that required great men to disregard personal danger and take risks for the sake of experience. He was also schooled by

GAUGAMELA FACTS

Who: Alexander the Great (356–323 BC) with 47,000 Greek/Macedonian troops versus 240,000 Persians under the Great King Darius (reigned 336–330 BC).

What: Alexander used an oblique formation to break the Persian front, Darius fled and the Persian army then collapsed.

Where: Near Tel Gomel, in what is now northern Iraq.

When: 1 October 331 BC.

Why: Alexander sought to finally defeat Darius in battle and complete his conquest of the Persian empire.

Outcome: Darius was murdered, possibly by his own generals. Alexander became master of Persia.

ALEXANDER LEADS HIS COMPANION CAVALRY *across the Granicus, seizing the initiative from the Persians. Like most successful military commanders, Alexander was no stranger to luck.*

nobility now had a requirement for military service and the army was a clear route to greatness. Philip lavished rewards on his officers and soldiers who distinguished themselves, and Alexander was not slow to notice the morale effects of his father's generosity.

Philip was murdered by one of his own bodyguards, and it is possible that Alexander was behind the plot. There are other explanations which are also plausible, and Alexander himself took the line that Persia was behind the murder of the King of Macedon. Alexander's succession was a typically messy business involving the murder or execution of potential rivals and enemies, and it had repercussions that lasted throughout Alexander's reign. He did not dwell over it, however, but immediately began his own campaign of conquest. Alexander's early campaigns were to subdue rebellions among tribles on his northern border and in Greece itself. As soon as he was able, he turned against Persia as he had always intended. A Macedonian force was already skirmishing in Persia, though little of importance had been achieved. In 334 BC Alexander reinforced this army and began his great campaign.

THE PERSIAN EMPIRE IN 334 BC

The Persian Empire was enormous, stretching all the way from the Mediterranean to the Indian Ocean. It was extremely wealthy but internally divided. The Persian Empire under Darius could field vast numbers of troops but these were drawn from many different regions and cultures. They had no common structure and in some cases spoke an entirely different language. Many of the troops of the empire were provided by subject peoples who resented their status and were not totally enthusiastic about fighting for their Great King. This created an additional problem – not only did Persia need to protect and control a huge area, some of the troops it fielded were not very reliable.

Some of Darius' troops were Greek mercenaries. This was common and often the mercenaries were more reliable than the forces of subject peoples that made up the great mass of Persian soldiery. These Greek mercenaries formed the backbone of the army that first opposed Alexander as he advanced into Asia Minor.

VICTORY AT THE GRANICUS

Alexander was an extremely aggressive commander who saw any sort of defensive preparation as a sign of weakness. He was therefore encouraged, rather than dismayed, when a Persian army drew up behind the river Granicus, forcing him to make an opposed crossing. Alexander declared that the

Aristotle himself in matters of philosophy and science, and was a charming host to court guests even as a boy. Aristotle was appointed, to a great extent, to curb Alexander's rashness and aggression or at least temper it with more philosophical and civilized values. In this he was not entirely successful.

Alexander learned a great deal from his tutor and became a very erudite man, but he remained essentially the boy who wanted to be Hercules. Hercules was Alexander's inspiration; Homer's tales of his deeds inspired Alexander in general attitude and some specific instances. It is likely that Alexander saw himself as a modern-day version of the classic Greek heroes. In many ways this was true.

At the time Alexander inherited the kingdom of Macedon, Philip II had made it the dominant power in Greek affairs. Athens, Thebes and even Sparta were eclipsed, and the Persians had been driven from Thrace. Alexander had been involved in some of the later campaigning and was making a name for himself as an aggressive, even reckless commander. Philip had also changed the nature of Macedonian society. The existing

Persians were not confident of victory and were counting on the steep riverbanks to break the force of his attack sufficiently for the Persian cavalry to defeat him. He hurled his cavalry across the river at the point where the enemy seemed strongest, and after a hard-fought mêlée was able to rout the Persian cavalry. The Persian second line, the Greek mercenaries, stood firm but were massacred.

The Granicus established the moral dominance of Alexander's army over his foes and forced Darius into an even more defensive mindset. Several cities of the region came over to Alexander and he was able to consolidate his conquest of the region without much interference. Only the fortified port of Halicarnassus put up much of a fight, and since no serious attempt to relieve it was made, the city eventually fell to Alexander's army.

Alexander's army was able to rapidly secure the whole region of Anatolia. The Persian army did not interfere, though local tribes caused some problems. Alexander advanced on Cilicia, from here he could strike either towards Egypt or directly at the Persian heartlands. Darius was finally forced to act.

Darius had assembled an army some 140,000 strong while Alexander was clearing his flank of holdout coastal cities and subduing hill barbarians. Alexander moved south into Syria to place his army across Darius' rear and Darius, entering Cilicia through mountain passes in the north, found himself positioned across Alexander's line of supply. Darius, still thinking defensively, chose a good position on the river Pinarus and awaited Alexander's next move. Alexander again interpreted this as a sign of nervousness and launched a head-on attack. Alexander fought on foot at

the head of his infantry and, as at Granicus, defeated the Persian force at the critical point. The Persian army disintegrated and the Macedonians pursued the remnants with great vigour. Darius himself escaped, though his family were captured.

THE LULL

During the next two years Alexander, who now held half the Persian Empire, reduced pockets of resistance and eliminated the Persian fleet's Mediterranean bases. He cheekily seized Egypt, trusting to Darius' defensive mentality to prevent an attack on his rear while he was campaigning to the west.

By the summer of 331 BC, Alexander was ready to complete his conquest of the Persian Empire. Vastly outnumbered and at the end of a long line of supply, he nevertheless decided that rather than accept Darius' offer to recognize his conquests he would stake all on an attempt to take the whole empire. This was Alexander's attitude in a nutshell – all or nothing. Advancing into Mesopotamia, the ancient cradle of civilization between the Tigris and the Euphrates rivers, Alexander offered his challenge to Darius, King of Kings. Darius considered retreating further into his territory and perhaps scorching the earth behind him, but instead decided to give battle.

DARIUS' PREPARATIONS

Darius knew that Alexander would need to give battle as soon as he could since he was operating at the end of a long supply line and the Persians were not. He chose his ground near the modern city of Mosul in Iraq and made his preparations for battle. Darius was determined to give

HORSE ARCHER VERSUS COMPANION CAVALRY

Mounted archers such as this Scythian (left) posed one of the Ancient Near East's most deadly threats to Western infantry, such as Greek hoplites, Alexander's phalanx, or Roman legionaries. Riding close to fire, into the ranks on foot, horse archers would then retire to a safe distance, at a speed made possible by a lack of any serious armour for the rider and the horse.

But pursuit by other cavalry could negate the threat of such archers. Alexander had his own Thracian cavalry ready, and successfully thwarted this Persian threat at Gaugamela.

Companion Cavalry (right) were literally that, the sons of the Macedonian nobility, raised along with Alexander under Philip's supervision and trained in the tactics Philip had learned from the Theban Epaminondas. Many of them were personal friends to whom he owed his life.

Companion Cavalry carried the shorter cavalry sarissa and lighter armor, and always fought under Alexander's personal command. To the cavalry was given the decisive role in Alexander's battles.

When the lumbering phalanx created a gap in the enemy's line, the cavalry would charge through and disrupt and destroy the enemy ranks by carrying out flanking attacks.

himself all the advantages, even though he commanded five times as many troops as Alexander. He ordered the ground flattened and obstructions removed to allow his cavalry and scythed chariots the best possible run at the enemy.

Darius' initial attack would be made by his first line, which was composed mostly of cavalry with a few of the best Persian infantry units mixed in. Darius himself was in the

A FOREST OF SPEARS – a frontal view of a Macedonian speira, the unit making up the larger infantry phalanx. The ranks behind the front five would hold their counter-weighted pikes aloft until required to fill a gap, and in the hope of deflecting incoming missiles.

centre of the Persian line with his 10,000-strong personal guard, who were known to the Greeks as the Immortals. In front of them were arrayed some 200 scythed chariots. A second line, composed of enormous numbers of infantry, was positioned behind the first. Darius expected to be able to envelop both of Alexander's flanks with his vastly superior numbers and to crush his army from all sides. Alexander's line

PAINTED IN 1673 by Charles Le Brun (1619–90) – a full 1800 years after the battle – 'The Battle of Gaugamela' (oil on canvas) is a highly romanticized depiction of the bloody confrontation between Darius's Persians and Alexander's Macedonians.

ENTITLED 'Alexander and the Family of Darius' (1708), this painting by Sebastiano Ricci shows Alexander meeting the widow and family of Darius folowing his victory over the Persians and triumphant march into Babylon.

would be punctured and broken by the onslaught of cavalry and chariots (and, according to some accounts) war elephants. The infantry would then advance to complete the victory. However, Alexander had other ideas.

BATTLE COMMENCES

To help protect his flanks from envelopment Alexander used a version of the oblique order of battle pioneered by the Thebans in 371 BC. He positioned the units of his cavalry on the flanks with each one echeloned back from the last, creating 'refused' flanks that required the enemy to move further if he wanted to engage them. His phalanx of well-drilled Macedonian infantry was positioned in the centre of the Greek line. A reserve phalanx formed Alexander's second line.

Alexander's plan called for his left flank, under the veteran general Parmenio, to fight a holding action while Alexander led the right wing to victory. He was assisted in this by the Persians themselves, who sent their left-flank cavalry far around Alexander's right, opening up a gap in their line. The Macedonian army was drifting to the right. If Darius delayed too long his chariots might not gain the benefit of their prepared run. So the attack was launched. Darius' cavalry swept around the flanks of the Macedonian force as the chariots (and, in some accounts, 15 war elephants) made their initial frontal attack.

The Macedonian line was able to fend off the chariots and weather the initial onslaught, though some of the Persian cavalry were able to break through. They were engaged by the reserve phalanx and by light troops, which had been briefed for the task. Some Persians began rifling the Macedonians' baggage train. If they had turned on the rear of the outnumbered and embattled Macedonians they might have contributed to a victory. Instead they took themselves out of the battle when they were most needed. As he had planned, Alexander led his elite Companion Cavalry and supported forces against the Persian left. Exploiting the gap that was opening between the Persian left wing cavalry and the centre, the Companions inflicted a savage blow on the forces in front of them. They were followed by a great wedge of infantry and light troops which fell on the disorganized Persians.

Fearing that he would be cut off, the commander of the Persian left wing, Bessus, began to retire which eased the pressure on Alexander's refused far right flank. Meanwhile, Darius himself was feeling the pressure. If Alexander's all-conquering cavalry wheeled his way instead of savaging Bessus, Darius himself might be surrounded and captured. Thoughts of previous defeats may have played heavily on the Persian emperor, for he, too, began to retreat. The withdrawal became a rout as Darius' bodyguards followed their leader in fleeing the field. Alexander was not able to pursue as the situation on his left was becoming desperate.

Parmenio's forces were hard-pressed on the left but had done their job, tying down the Persians' force. Now Alexander fell upon the rear of the Persians engaging Parmenio, forcing them to retreat. The Persian right-wing commander, Mazaeus, tried to conduct an orderly retreat but was vigorously attacked and his troops thrown into confusion.

This represented the end of organized Persian resistance at Gaugamela. The remaining Persian forces were scattered, chased off or cut down and the baggage train was captured. Alexander began a three-day pursuit of Darius' surviving forces but was unable to catch his enemy, who regrouped much of his surviving cavalry and a few thousand infantry and made good his escape. Behind the fleeing Darius were left 40,000 dead Persian troops, 4000 more as prisoners and the remainder of the army scattered about the countryside.

AFTERMATH

Gaugamela was a decisive defeat for Darius. He retained his crown and part of his army, but was unable to pose any challenge to Alexander, who pushed on into Persia itself. Taking Susa, he drove on to the capital Persepolis and made himself master of the Persian Empire in all but title. With Darius alive he could not claim the title.

Darius evaded capture, finally, reaching the friendly kingdom of Bactria where he was found dead, murdered. Finally, the Persians could surrender. Alexander was proclaimed 'Great King' and added Persia to his growing empire. Alexander's reign would eventually extend to India.

GAUGAMELA

3 The Persian left tries to outflank the Macedonians, but they cannot get past the light troops and cavalry.

1 The Macedonian phalanx marches obliquely towards the Persian line. The Persian chariots are repulsed by javelins.

4 Alexander and the Companions break through a weak spot in the Persian line and swing leftwards.

2 Darius' secret weapons, his Indian war elephants and scythe-armed chariots, prove to be a disappointment.

5 Some Persians break through the phalanx, but they head to the rear to attack the Macedonian baggage train.

6 The Greek left wing is hard-pressed by the Persian cavalry until Alexander appears in the latter's rear.

KEY
MACEDONIANS
PERSIANS

7 Darius, fearing for his safety, decides to flee from the battlefield, effectively giving the victory to Alexander.

CANNAE

Hannibal's destruction of a Roman army at Cannae by a brilliant double envelopment provided a model for commanders for centuries to come. But even this, the third of his great tactical victories over the Roman Republic, did not end the Punic Wars.

After their defeat in the First Punic War (264–241 BC) the Carthaginians began trying to expand and develop possessions in Spain to make good territorial losses in Sicily and Sardinia. Much of this was carried out by the Barca family, especially Hamilcar, the distinguished young general of the first war with Rome and his son, Hannibal. Under the Barcas, the Carthaginians extracted the mineral and manpower resources that Spain had to offer them.

The Romans watched the Carthaginian subjugation of Spain with a certain amount of trepidation and so, in 226 BC, a treaty was concluded that placed Spain south of the Ebro River in the Carthaginian sphere of influence and leaving the territory to the north in the Roman sphere. But the treaty was to be short-lived. By 221 BC the Carthaginian empire had (once again) become wealthy and rebuilt its

CANNAE FACTS

Who: Hannibal Barca (247–183 or 182 BC) with a Carthaginian army of 50,000 men faced the Roman consuls Paullus and Varro with an army of 86,000 men.

What: Hannibal made the most of his advantage in cavalry and planned a double envelopment of the Romans. He weakened his infantry centre and strengthened his wings with good infantry and cavalry.

Where: At the mouth of the River Aufidius in Apulia, Italy.

When: 2 August 216 BC.

Why: Hannibal had invaded Italy to weaken Rome by separating her from her Italian allies.

Outcome: The battle was a devastating tactical defeat for the Romans with more than 48,000 killed and 20,000 prisoners. Although the battle had a profound psychological effect on the Romans for centuries to come, the strategic advantages of Roman manpower and stalwart allies minimized the overall impact of the battle.

THIS NINETEENTH-CENTURY ILLUSTRATION *shows Hannibal and his army stripping the defeated Romans of arms and armour after their victory at Cannae.*

THIS SPANISH CHIEFTAIN wears a fine bronze helmet, the colour of reddish brass, and a mail shirt. The links were individually forged and riveted together – very expensive. He rides a small horse. Modern research shows the lack of stirrups would not affect his ability to throw his spear or strike downwards against infantry in a mêlée.

HANNIBAL ENTERING A NORTHERN ITALIAN TOWN on elephantback in triumph. Elephants had helped Hannibal in his crossing of the Alps, but once the Roman troops and cavalry became inured to these strange beasts, they were relatively ineffective on the battlefield.

army, composed mainly of Carthage's Libyan subjects, Numidian mercenaries and levies from subject Spanish tribes. At this time, the Carthaginians, led by Hannibal, supported one of their allies against Saguntum, a town located south of the Ebro, and besieged and took the town in late 219 or early 218 BC. Unfortunately, the Romans claimed a pre-existing alliance with Saguntum and demanded that the Carthaginians desist and turn Hannibal over to them. The outraged Carthaginians responded that they would do no such thing and so the Second Punic War began.

THE SECOND PUNIC WAR

Hannibal quickly took the offensive and launched an invasion of Italy with an army of 59,000 men including 9000 cavalry. He moved quickly and thereby avoided Roman efforts to intercept him in Gaul. The swift passage of his army was not, however, without consequences and Hannibal entered Italy in November of 218 BC with a force that was greatly weakened by campaigning – only 6000 cavalry and 20,000 infantry had survived the passage over the Alps. The Carthaginian strategy was for Hannibal to quickly seek battle and he won a cavalry skirmish at the Ticinus River and the Romans were forced to withdraw. The following month, Hannibal fought the set-piece battle of the war when he lured a Roman army across the River Trebia. Pinning the Romans with his infantry, Hannibal used his superior cavalry and a hidden force to attack the Romans in the flanks and rear respectively. The Romans were decisively routed, losing perhaps three-quarters of their 40,000 men as casualties or prisoners of war.

Hannibal was in control of northern Italy and in the spring of 217 BC began his march into central and then southern Italy. Although the Romans tried to keep Hannibal and his army contained in the north, he managed to slip by them. The Carthaginians were pursued by a Roman army and, along the shores of Lake Trasimene on 21 June, Hannibal sprung an ambush on the Roman troops. Caught between the lake and the Carthaginians, the Roman army was smashed losing perhaps 15,000 men.

FABIUS MAXIMUS

Having suffered two major defeats, the Romans took the unusual step of suspending their constitution, under which the state and army were controlled by two annually elected consuls, and elected a dictator who would prosecute the war with supreme power for a period of six months. The man elected was Quintus Fabius Maximus. Fabius devised a strategy based upon the Romans avoiding battle with Hannibal while shadowing his army. This 'Fabian Strategy' allowed the Romans to trade space for time while making it difficult for Hannibal to disperse his forces during the winter. Since the Romans and their allies controlled most of the towns, this posed some logistical difficulties on the Carthaginians. Hannibal had hoped that his victories would convince many of Rome's Italian allies to abandon her, but in fact most remained steadfast in their loyalty to the Romans. Moreover, time favoured the Romans in that it allowed them and their allies to muster a large army from their significant reserves, estimated to be more than three-quarters of a million men. The Roman army was composed of citizen soldiers who were conscripted annually to train and prepare for the coming battle with the Carthaginians. The Romans followed Hannibal's army into Apulia, Samnium and Campania. The strategy seemed to be working since Fabius' second-in-command was even able to inflict a defeat on the Carthaginians in a major skirmish while the latter were dispersed in order to forage. The Romans, however, were not happy with Fabius' strategy, especially since Hannibal had, on more than one occasion, been able to outmanoeuvre the Romans when they seemingly had him contained.

THE CAMPAIGN AND THE ARMIES

Although Fabius' term as dictator expired at the end of 217 BC, his successors basically continued to avoid Hannibal, waiting for reinforcements to arrive under the new consuls for the year 216 BC. The new consuls were Lucius Aemilius Paullus and Gaius Terentius Varro. Paullus was a man of some considerable military experience who had seen action fighting against the Illyrians and had held the consulship on

A NUMIDIAN LIGHT CAVALRYMAN from around 200 BC. He is armed with a javelin and small shield. These horsemen were such good riders that they had no need of a bridle to control the horse.

a previous occasion. He had even been awarded a triumph for the campaign. Varro was less experienced but was apparently a popular politician with much support amongst both the aristocracy and the common folk. The consuls, elected in March, had spent the spring raising additional troops and joined the army watching Hannibal in Apulia sometime in July. When they arrived, the army under their command was the largest the Romans had ever put in the field. It was composed of eight legions, 40,000 infantry and 2400 cavalry, and an equal number of Italian allies, totaling 40,000 on foot and 3600 on horses. About half of the Roman force probably had some experience but the remainder were freshly-levied troops with only modest training, who had not seen combat.

ROMAN LEGIONARY

Roman infantry knew what was expected of it and was given the means to fulfill the Republic's demands. The long hasta in this legionary's hand marks him as one of the *hastati*, the third line of the Roman legion that held the formation in place while the *principes* and *triarii* changed position in the front of the formation. His bronze helmet and greaves show more Greek influence than would those worn by his successors. A laminated scutum of wood and leather strips has not yet reached its full evolutionary weight of 7.5kg (16.5lbs).

CANNAE

1 Paullus deploys close to the river to restrict the movement of Hannibal's superior cavalry in the battle.

4 The Roman cavalry are met by the Gallic and Spanish cavalry, some of whom fight dismounted. The Roman cavalry flee.

7 The Gallic and Spanish cavalry now remount, and ride to strike the Roman allied cavalry in the rear.

6 Hannibal's African troops now attack the Roman legions in the flank, as the Gauls and Spanish rally.

5 The Roman legions press back the Gallic and Spanish infantry, drawing in more and more men.

KEY

CATHAGINIANS

ROMANS

9 The Gallic and Spanish cavalry then seal the Romans' fate by striking them in the rear, leaving them surrounded.

8 The allied cavalry, having held off Hannibal's Numidians, now break as the Gauls and Spaniards attack their rear.

3 The Roman and Carthaginian light troops begin the battle.

2 Hannibal deploys in a crescent formation.

ALESIA

52 BC

Caesar's victory at Alesia, where Roman skill at military engineering enabled him to defeat a vast Gallic army coming to relieve their chieftain Vercingetorix, besieged in the town, secured Roman rule in Gaul. But for all his fortifications, Caesar had a hard fight of it.

In 59 BC, Gaius Julius Caesar was elected consul in Rome. He used his position and political connections to secure his appointment as the governor of Cisalpine and Transalpine Gaul and Illyricum at the conclusion of his consulship. He took up the governorship the following year and used the migration of the Helvetii, and the trepidation this caused amongst Rome's Gallic allies, as a pretext to intervene militarily in Gaul. While it does not seem that Caesar initially intended to conquer Gaul, his victory over the Helvetii may have provided him with the opportunity to contemplate doing so. Over the next five years Caesar waged a number of successful, if sometimes close-run, campaigns in Gaul, forcing many tribes to submit to him, at least temporarily. Moreover, Caesar also launched campaigns across the Rhine and twice invaded Britain.

ALESIA FACTS

Who: Gaius Julius Caesar (100–44 BC), with an army of 45,000 men, besieged an army of around 70,000 Gauls under Vercingetorix of the Arverni (d. 46 BC) and faced a relief force reputed to number 250,000 warriors.

What: Caesar made use of the Roman skill at siege warfare by constructing lines of siege works facing both inward and outward and Roman discipline to defeat threats from both the besieged and relieving forces.

Where: Alesia, some 48km (30 miles) northwest of modern Dijon in France.

When: Late September/early October 52 BC.

Why: Caesar sought to defeat Vercingetorix's threat to Roman rule once and for all.

Outcome: The battle was the last major effort by the Gauls against Caesar. The defeat of the charismatic Vercingetorix and the sizeable forces mustered for the battle ended the Gauls' ability to resist the Romans.

LEGIONARIES CONSTRUCT DEFENSIVE WORKS. The Roman army were unparalleled in the ancient world as builders of small fortresses. They were also highly skilled at building defensive walls.

43

During the construction of the fortifications, Vercingetorix made a number of substantial and coordinated sorties from the town, which interfered with construction and made it difficult for Caesar to send out foragers. He therefore added three lines of traps to make enemy attack more difficult. The first consisted of five rows of sharpened tree trunks and stout branches set in trenches, in front of them were pits 90cm (3ft) deep arranged in the fashion of a chessboard, with sharpened stakes set inside, and in front, iron hooks set in wooden blocks were scattered about.

In order to defend against the relief army a similar set of fortifications 28km (17 miles) in length were built facing outwards with plenty of room in between for Caesar to move his troops. Caesar also had his men collect a one-month reserve of food and fodder. The Gauls within Alesia recognized that supplies would become short so they sent out of the town all of those who were not able to fight. The non-combatants went to the Roman lines but were turned away by Caesar and so were left to starve in a no-man's land.

A RECONSTRUCTION OF THE LORICA segmentata showing how the iron segments are held together with hooks and riveted leather straps to produce a flexible yet effective armour.

THE BATTLE

The battle began as the relief force arrived and, after having camped within a mile of the Roman lines, sent out their cavalry into a 4.8km (3-mile) wide plain. The Gallic horse

'VERCINGETORIX THROWING HIS WEAPONS AT THE FEET OF CÈSAR', Lionel-Noël Royer's (1852–1926) depiction of Vercingetorix offers a romanticized view of the Gallic leader's surrender. Caesar is depicted dressed as a political figure rather than a soldier.

had archers and light infantry interspersed, while the main body of infantry formed up to watch their cavalry who were the elite of the army. When the Gauls within Alesia saw the cavalry formed for battle, they came out of the town and started to fill in the Roman trenches with fascines in preparation for a sortie. Caesar responded by manning the ramparts with all of his infantry, making sure that each man knew his post, and sending out his Gallic allied and German horse to meet the enemy cavalry. The cavalry action was fiercely contested, the Gallic horse benefiting from the support of the infantry in their midst, something the Romans had not expected. The fighting lasted from noon until sunset, but eventually the Romans had the better of it when Caesar massed his German cavalry at a single point and they broke the Gallic cavalry. The latter fled leaving their infantry supports to be slaughtered and were pursued back to their camp. The Gauls within the siege works despaired and retired back to Alesia.

The Gauls of the relief force spent the following day preparing the materials needed for a major assault, including ladders, grappling hooks and fascines. At midnight, they quietly advanced and, once near the Roman siege works, gave a shout to let the besieged know they were beginning the assault. As a result Vercingetorix led out his forces to attack the Romans at the same time so that the Romans would be engaged to front and rear. Although the Gauls were able to cause a number of casualties by hurling javelins, slinging stones and others missiles, the obstacles set up by the Romans before their ramparts made it extremely difficult and caused heavy losses. The Gauls were unable to penetrate the Roman lines and, fearing a counter-attack, therefore retreated.

The Gauls held a council of war and decided to use the main army to threaten the siege works while a force of 60,000 picked men attacked a Roman camp on the north side of the town. This fort was defended by two legions, but due to the nature of the terrain, it lay outside of the lines of circumvallation. Meanwhile Vercingetorix would again lead an attack so the Romans would be forced to defend both the inner and outer defences against simultaneous assaults. The Gallic force of warriors marched through the night and rested until noon at which point they attacked. At the same time Vercingetorix attacked the inward-facing fortifications so that the Romans were hard pressed at several places. Caesar noticed that the 60,000 Gauls were having some success against the isolated fort and so he sent his most trusted lieutenant, Titus Atius Labienus, to its relief with six cohorts. He ordered Labienus to defend the fort but if it appeared he could no longer defend it, he should instead counter-attack. In the meantime, Vercingetorix's troops had breached a steep section of the inner wall where the fortifications were not as complete.

Caesar sent reinforcements to this position, eventually repulsing the Gauls when he personally led some troops to the breach. By this point the situation had become desperate and Labienus was preparing for a last-ditch counter-attack. Caesar rushed to aid the counter-attack leading a mere four cohorts, but he also ordered his cavalry to sally out and assault the Gallic warriors from behind. Although the Gauls

GALLIC WARRIOR

The archetypal barbarian warrior with bare chest, fierce moustache and patterned trousers. The Gallic tribesman was a dangerous foe. Roman writers such as Tacitus praised their courage and stoicism. Gauls had defeated Roman armies on previous occasions, but their main weakness was a lack of good organization. Where the Roman army was a well-drilled and obedient body of professional troops, the Gallic force facing it was a loose collection of proud and aggressive men bound together by ties of personal, tribal and family loyalties. In a short campaign or while they were winning this was not a problem, but once supplies became an issue and victory was doubtful there was a tendency for Gallic armies to break up and groups to begin to drift away.

put up a fight, the appearance of cavalry behind them was too much and they were routed. The Roman cavalry were able to cause tremendous casualties amongst the routing Gauls. The besieged Gauls were dismayed by this turn of events and retired into Alesia.

AFTERMATH

With the rout of the relief army, the Gauls within Alesia were forced to surrender. Vercingetorix was handed over to Caesar. Some of the Gauls were used to help gain the loyalty of their tribes but many were distributed to the troops as booty and ended up as slaves. The victory at Alesia effectively broke Gallic resistance, although Caesar would spend the next two years consolidating his position. Vercingetorix would remain a prisoner for some six years until, after having been paraded in Rome during Caesar's great triumph, he was publicly strangled.

ALESIA

5 A large relief army of about 250,000 men arrives, and makes three serious attempts to lift the siege of the town.

KEY

ROMAN ARMY

GALLIC FORCES

6 The men inside Alesia coordinate their attacks with the relief army, but are defeated by Caesar's Germanic cavalry.

1 Vercingetorix and approximately 70,000 soldiers take refuge in the fortified hilltop town of Alesia.

4 The women and children are forced out of Alesia to save food, and have to camp between the two forces.

2 After the Gallic cavalry escapes, Caesar builds inner and outer walls of approximately 28km (17.4 miles) in length.

3 Forts are constructed along the walls with plenty of space between them to move troops to trouble spots.

ADRIANOPLE AD 378

Described by the soldier and historian Amminaus Marcellinus as the worst Roman military disaster since Cannae, the Battle of Adrianople saw the field army of the Eastern Roman Empire virtually destroyed and the Emperor killed. But the Goths were unable to fully exploit this success thanks to the fortifications of Constantinople.

In AD 376, two Visigothic chieftains, Fritigern and Alavivus, made a request to the Eastern Roman Emperor Valens to cross the Danube and settle on the Roman side of that great river. The reason behind the request lay to the east. The Goths were being pressured by a migration of steppe nomads, the Huns, who were on the move westwards, driving the Goths and other Germanic groups before them. Valens agreed to the Goths' request with the stipulation that the Visigoths surrender their arms and convert to Christianity, both of which were acceptable to the Gothic leaders. Valens' reasons for allowing the Visigoths within the empire were that they would provide the imperial army with a valuable source of recruits and that he could then transmute the

ADRIANOPLE FACTS

Who: The Eastern Roman Emperor Valens (d. AD 378) with an army of 20,000 men faced a slightly smaller army of Goths under Fritigern.

What: The Goths took advantage of the impetuous advance by the Romans and the serendipitous arrival of the Gothic cavalry (who had been away foraging) to catch the Romans between the Gothic fortified wagon laager and their returning Gothic horsemen.

Where: Near Adrianople in Thrace.

When: 9 August AD 378.

Why: The Goths, driven west by the Huns, invaded Thrace to take by force supplies the Romans had promised them but withheld.

Outcome: The battle was a devastating tactical defeat for the Romans who lost two-thirds of the eastern field army.

THIS DRAMATIC DETAIL from the Ludovisi Sarcophagus (c. 250–260 AD), shows Roman troops in a life or death struggle with barbarian invaders.

ADRIANOPLE

4 More returning Gothic cavalry assault the Roman left flank, already in disarray after their abortive attack.

2 While negotiations are going on, Roman cavalry on the left flank probe the Gothic defences, only to be driven back in disorder.

6 Gothic cavalry strike the Roman infantry on both flanks, rapidly surrounding and annihilating the Roman centre.

KEY

◀ VISIGOTHS

◀ ROMANS

1 As the Romans approach, the Goths adopt a defensive position, circling their wagons into laagers to protect women and children and manning the makeshift defence with infantry.

3 The Gothic cavalry return from a foraging expedition and fall on the Roman right flank.

5 The Roman cavalry are driven from the field in disorder.

TOURS/POITIERS

AD 732

The battle of Tours/Poitiers was a turning point in world history that decided the fate of Western Europe. It was here that the tide of Muslim conquest was turned back, with enormous implications for the future of the entire world.

After the fall of the Western Roman Empire, Europe fragmented into many small kingdoms and tribal groupings. This era has been called the 'Dark Ages' but in fact culture and civilization flourished in most areas. However, it was a turbulent time in which many successors to Roman power fought one another and battled barbarians along their frontiers. By AD 700, several large kingdoms had arisen. Spain was more or less dominated by the Visigoths, who had migrated there from the east. The Duchy of Aquitaine ruled southwestern France. But by far the largest of the western European states was the kingdom of the Franks, which stretched from the

TOURS/POITIERS FACTS

Who: A force of Franks under Charles Martel (AD 688–741), versus a superior army of Muslim Moorish cavalry under Emir Abd-ar-Rahman (d. AD 732).

What: The Frankish infantry established itself in a defensive position and awaited attack by the Moorish cavalry. After a hard-fought battle the Franks emerged victorious.

Where: Between modern Tours and Poitiers in France.

When: 10 October AD 732.

Why: Muslim forces had taken Iberia and were spilling over the Pyrenees to conquer

more of Europe. They were opposed by the Christian Franks.

Outcome: A decisive victory for the Franks. Charles Martel made his reputation in this battle. The Moorish commander was killed and his army retired to Spain.

THIS DRAMATIC NINETEENTH-CENTURY *painting by Carl von Steuben (1788-1856) depicts Charles Martel's stand at Tours/Poitiers. Although somewhat romanticized, the painting conveys the desperate nature of close-quarters fighting.*

English Channel and North Sea coasts to the Mediterranean, and from a narrow holding on the Atlantic coast north of Aquitaine to Bavaria and Saxony.

The Frankish kingdom was a Christian state, like most of Europe, and could field a powerful army based around a core of élite armoured infantry and bound to their leader by oaths and family bonds. The remainder of the force was made up of lighter-armed footsoldiers; armoured cavalry were not yet the dominant force in European warfare, though their day was coming soon.

The Franks were powerful and warlike. No less martial, but far less potent, was the Visigothic kingdom of Iberia, which by AD 700 was in dire straits. With famine in some areas and the nobility fighting among themselves, central authority had broken down and rivals of the king, Roderick, decided that the time was ripe for a takeover. Roderick's

THE FRANKS ENTERED the Arab camp late in the battle. The infiltration and looting of their camp was a major factor in weakening the Muslim's assault on the Frankish positions.

rivals turned for aid to what was probably the greatest power of the era, the Umayyad (or Omayyad) Caliphate, the vast Muslim empire that stretched all along the north coast of Africa through Egypt, Arabia and on to Mesopotamia. In AD 711, assistance was granted by Tariq ibd Ziyad, governor of Tangiers, in the form of 10,000 troops. With their Visigothic allies, this force landed at Gibraltar and so began the Muslim conquest of Iberia. Defeating Roderick in battle, the Muslim forces rapidly conquered much of the country. Whether or not they had initially intended to help Roderick's opponents, they now set about making themselves masters of Iberia.

EXPEDITIONS INTO EUROPE

After the initial invasion, Tariq ibd Ziyad was superseded in command by his superior, a member of the Umayyad dynasty, named Musa ibn Unsay. Ever-larger forces entered Iberia and turned it into a province of the Caliphate. Some areas were overrun but retained a degree of autonomy, retaining their religious freedom, such as the principality of Murcia, while other regions, notably Asturias, held out as best they could or revolted against Umayyad rule.

Some of those holding out were in the Pyrenees, between what is now France and Spain. Expeditions were sent against them, and ultimately through the mountains against the kingdoms there, which were thought to be supporting the rebels. As the Muslims crossed the mountains and began making forays into Europe, alarm grew. By AD 720 Moorish forces had a toe-hold in southern France and were expanding their control. They launched raids as far as the Rhône valley.

A series of internal problems and revolts slowed Muslim expansion into Europe for several years, but in AD 730 the then leader, Abd-ar-Rahman, launched an expedition into Aquitaine to remove the threat to his northern border. Defeating the Aquitainians at Bordeaux, Rahman's army rampaged through the Duchy of Aquitaine, breaking its power and reducing its strongholds.

The neighbouring Frankish kingdom had several princes with various titles, but the greatest of them, ruler of the Franks in all but name, was Charles. It was in the coming campaign that the Frankish prince earned his title Martel, which means 'The Hammer'. Born in what is now Belgium, Charles Martel had been previously imprisoned to prevent succession complications. This was not entirely successful. He escaped and during the ensuing civil war he learned the value of, what today would be called, logistics. After a shaky start he emerged as a wily and surprisingly modern commander. Coming to the field with forces capable of winning the battle was part of his pattern of strategy. He also learned the value of striking unexpectedly and of defying convention when it was advantageous to do so. The great

Chinese military thinker Sun Tzu, of whom Charles of course had never heard, would recognize many of his tactics. His military brilliance allowed Charles Martel to create a unified kingdom under his rule, though he did not take the title of king. By AD 732 Charles was an enormously powerful figure in Europe. He was also popular with the Church as a champion of Christianity.

Who better, then, to lead the Christian Franks in repelling the invaders and their foreign religion? In fact Charles had been preparing to do just that for some years. Although he did engage in various campaigns between AD 720 and 732, he was well aware of the threat from the southeast and had begun to create an army to defeat it. This is typical of the man – he did not rush in to fight his foes but instead worked out how they could be beaten before offering battle. The core of Charles' strategy against the invaders was the creation of a force of élite heavy infantry who were professionals capable of training all year round. This was not the practice of the time; other than small bodyguards, fighting men were normally raised for a campaign then went home to their farms afterwards.

Charles equipped his professionals lavishly and protected them with good armour. He trained them well and allowed them to gain experience in combat, increasing their confidence and steadiness. He did have some mounted troops but cavalry was not much in use in Europe at that time and they lacked stirrups. These mounted soldiers, who were not true cavalry and could not stand against the excellent horsemen of the Moorish Caliphate, were used as a mobile reserve or simply dismounted to fight.

THE CAMPAIGN OPENS

The Moorish forces were over-confident. They had easily beaten everything that Europe could put in their path and did not rate the 'barbarians' as fighters or as an army. Although a previous expedition had been defeated before the walls of Toulouse, the Muslims did not believe that Europe could offer any significant opposition.

The victor of Toulouse, Duke Odo of Aquitaine, met the Moors at the River Garonne and attempted to turn back the invasion. This time, however, there was to be no European victory. Large numbers of Berber (North African) and Arab cavalry crashed into Odo's army, which was scattered and ridden down. Suffering massive casualties, Odo's force ceased to be a factor in the campaign and the Muslims pushed on.

However, victories like Garonne contributed to the general over-confidence of the Moorish host. Scouting was neglected and victory became an expectation rather than something won by hard endeavour. This allowed Charles to choose the battleground and achieve a measure of surprise over his opponents, who were unaware of the size or quality of his force. Charles marched his force to intercept the Muslims, who he knew were on their way to attack Tours.

MUSLIM CAVALRY *from the invasion of Spain in the eighth century through to the Battle of Nicopolis in 1396 were generally less heavily armoured than their Christian counterparts and relied more on skirmishing than the full frontal charge.*

A FRANKISH SHIELDWALL. This spear-bristling phalanxe-style formation was powerful on the defensive, but only if it could maintain its cohesion. If it was broken, a slaughter often ensued.

He did not use the Roman roads, even though these offered the easiest going, as he expected these to be watched, but placed his force in the path of the opposing army. The exact location is unclear but lay somewhere between Poitiers and Tours, hence the fact that the battle is known to historians by two names.

The advancing Muslims stumbled upon Charles' force in its blocking position and were both surprised and nonplussed. Their scouts had brought no word of this force and it had simply appeared in their path. The Moorish leader, Emir Abd-ar-Rahman, hesitated to attack and sought to discover as much as possible as he could about these latest adversaries. The pause, which lasted six days, allowed Rahman to observe the enemy and to pull in his patrols and detached forces, but it also acted in the Franks' favour. The enemy were operating far from home in a colder climate than they were used to whilst the Franks were on home ground. It was obvious that Rahman was going to have to attack and the Franks were ready for him. They occupied a good defensive position and

could remain there indefinitely. Sooner or later, Rahman would have to attack or else turn around and go home.

THE MOORS CHARGE

Rahman had under his command between 40,000 and 60,000 cavalry who had carried before their charge every opponent they had met. Many of their defeated foes had been Frankish infantry like those arrayed before them. Any misgivings Rahman might have felt about charging uphill against a solid defensive formation were outweighed by his confidence in his cavalry. Or perhaps he simply felt that having come this far he could not simply retire. Subsequent events showed the value of discipline and confidence in battle. Conventional wisdom of the time said that infantry could not defeat cavalry, but Charles' troops did just that.

The Franks were drawn up in a large defensive square formation with reserve units inside. The capabilities of the infantry square were well proven at Tours.

The Moorish cavalry made several charges at Charles' square and, despite being tired by their heavy armour and the slope they attacked up, despite their formations being disrupted by the uneven ground and the trees that dotted it, they crashed home again and again.

CRISIS POINT

Several times groups of Moorish horsemen fought their way into the square. If they could establish themselves there it was all over; attack from within and without the square would mean that it would lose its cohesion and its scattered members be ridden down. Reserve forces within the square fell on them – infantry rushed confidently up to attack armoured cavalry, something that rarely happened and even less often successful – and killed them or drove them out of the square.

FRANKISH WARRIOR

A Frankish warrior armed with sword and shield. Armor was available to some well off warriors but most had to make do with a helmet and skilled use of their shield.

Matters were in some doubt for a time as the square was heavily beset from all sides, but then the pressure began to ease. Moorish warriors began falling back to their camp, leaving the square battered but intact.

RAHMAN KILLED

Some of Martel's scouts had managed to get into the Moorish camp during the battle, taking advantage of poor scouting and over-confidence on the part of the enemy. There, they freed prisoners and generally caused mayhem. This confusion in their rear, coupled with the worry that their hard-won plunder might be stolen back by the Franks, drew many of Rahman's troops back to the camp and severely disrupted the attack on the Franks' square. Rahman tried to stop the rearward movement but in so doing exposed himself with an inadequate bodyguard. He was killed by Frankish soldiers. The Moors were dismayed and retired in some disorder. The Franks tidied up their formation and remained in their defensive positions.

There was no clear successor to Rahman, and the Moorish force fell into disarray. The force began to retire in the direction of Iberia, though this was not immediately apparent to the Franks who suspected a feigned retreat to draw them off the hill they occupied. The Moors retained the means to defeat the Franks; they were still very powerful. However, its will had been broken and the various sub-commanders, still unable to agree who should take over, decided to continue their journey home. They had gained a considerable amount of plunder and still had much of it; little would be gained by a renewal of hostilities, or so they reasoned.

AFTERMATH

The battle of Tours/Poitiers has at times been lauded as the only reason Europe is not a Muslim state and a part of the Arab Empire. While this is an exaggeration, it is fair to say that Charles deserved the nickname 'The Hammer', or Martel, which was conferred on him for handing the Muslim expansion such a dramatic defeat.

Tours/Poitiers represented something of a high-water mark in the Muslim invasion of Europe. Expeditions over the Pyrenees would continue and Charles Martel would oppose them for the rest of his life. He would, in time, create the great Carolingian dynasty that produced Charlemagne, who is considered to be the father of European chivalry.

The Muslim occupation of Iberia continued for many centuries and advantage ebbed and flowed between Muslim and Christian forces in southwestern Europe. Charles Martel's victory did not end the Moorish invasion nor make invasion into further territory impossible. It was, however, the point where the easy Muslim victories ended and the long struggle began.

A WATERCOLOUR DEPICTION of Charles Martel's victory at Tours/Poitiers. This was not only the turning point of the Muslim invasion of western Europe, it also marked the emergence of the great Carolingian dynasty.

ANDALUCIAN HORSE ARCHER

The Muslim forces made great use of horse archers. Combining excellent mobility with good striking power, horse archers could choose when and where to attack and could often evade an enemy counterstroke. By skirmishing, they could erode an opposing force by wearing down and tiring out the troops, and by concentrating at a decisive point they could soften up a formation for assault by other units. Predominantly infantry forces had no effective counter to the hit-and-run tactics of the horse archers.

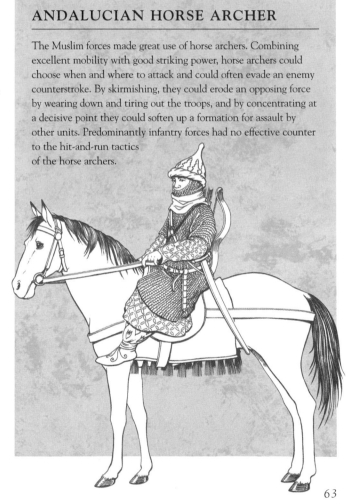

TOURS/POITIERS

3 Close-quarters fighting ensues. Penetrations of the Frankish formation are sealed and dealt with by reserve forces.

4 As repeated charges fail, word comes that the Franks are attacking the Muslim camp.

6 Demoralized and leaderless, the Muslim forces retreat to Spain leaving the Franks victorious.

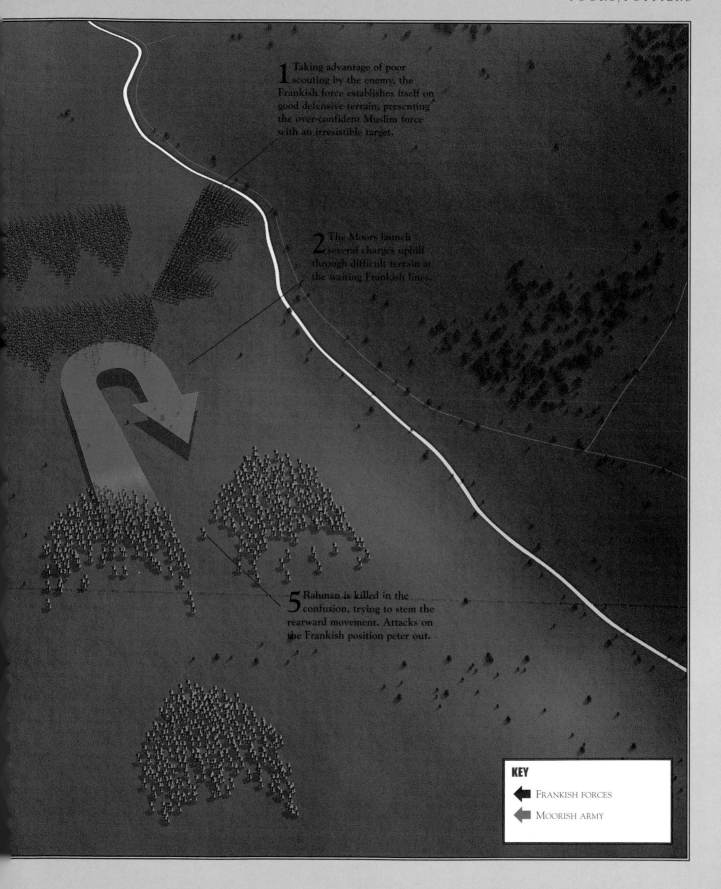

1 Taking advantage of poor scouting by the enemy, the Frankish force establishes itself on good defensive terrain, presenting the over-confident Muslim force with an irresistible target.

2 The Moors launch several charges uphill through difficult terrain at the waiting Frankish lines.

5 Rahman is killed in the confusion, trying to stem the rearward movement. Attacks on the Frankish position peter out.

KEY

FRANKISH FORCES

MOORISH ARMY

HASTINGS 1066

Norman mounted men-at-arms met the Anglo-Saxon shield wall in the longest, hardest-fought and most decisive battle in England in the early Middle Ages. William the Conqueror's victory changed English history forever, and ushered in the dominance of the mounted knight in European warfare.

In traditional accounts Harold's reputation was blackened as an oath-breaker, while others viewed William as the villain. It is probably safe to say that both of these remarkably able and ruthless men had their good and bad sides. William was the illegitimate son of the Duke of Normandy and he had to defend his position as Duke, from 1035 onwards, against all comers and by the time he wished to invade England had carved out the most powerful duchy in France and northwestern Europe, reducing both Brittany and Maine to vassal states. His influence was also predominant in Paris, where he dominated the young King Philip, and he had created a crucial ally in Flanders by marrying Matilda, the daughter of Duke Baldwin IV.

HASTINGS FACTS

Who: William, Duke of Normandy (1028–87), invaded England with an army of 6000 men to lay claim to the throne of King Harold II Godwinson (1022–66), who faced him with an army of 6300.

What: Norman cavalry and archers eventually wore down the Saxon shield wall formation.

Where: Senlac Ridge, 11.2km (7 miles) north of the town of Hastings, England.

When: 14 October 1066.

Why: William wanted to conquer England.

Outcome: Harold and most of the Anglo-Saxon nobility were killed, and William secured the throne of England.

THIS DRAMATIC DEPICTION *of the battle of Hastings by R. Caton Woodville shows King Harold Godwinson making his final stand against the Normans on Senlac Hill.*

THE NORMAN ARMY AS DISPLAYED IN THE BAYEUX TAPESTRY consists of cavalry and archers. Other contemporary sources indicate that the cavalry greatly outnumbered the archers, but the latter's role in the death of King Harold Godwinson no doubt accounts for their exaggerated presence.

William's claim to the English throne was very tenuous and lacked solid legal foundations. William had forced his rival, Harold Godwinson, in 1064 to swear an oath to leave Edward the Confessor's throne to him. But Harold had no intention of honouring an oath forced upon him through blackmail and threats. As the Earl of Wessex, vice-regent under Edward since 1064, the elderly King's brother-in-law, and with undoubted ability and good character, no man had a stronger or more legitimate claim to the throne of England. As a consequence when Edward died, on 5 January 1066, Harold was crowned in Westminster Abbey.

STAMFORD BRIDGE

Harold was no fool and he knew that the ruthlessly ambitious William would use his 'breaking' of the 'oath' as a spurious excuse to invade. Until May there was no threat of invasion but during the early summer William unleashed an ambitious naval building programme to create an armada of 500 ships to carry his 6000-strong army (of Normans, Bretons, French and Flemings) across the Channel.

In response Harold mobilized his 4000-strong Royal Guard, known by their Scandinavian name of huscarls, and the territorial Saxon militia, the fyrd. The fyrd could, in theory and given time, resources and money, mobilize 15,000–20,000 men but during the summer of 1066 it probably numbered no more than 4000. Harold strung out his army of 8000 men along the south coast waiting for the Normans. Harold ordered the fyrd to be disbanded on 8 September so that these men could return to their farms and gather in the all-important harvest. Unfortunately Harold had acted precipitously since news arrived that his brother, Earl Tostig, had joined forces with King Harald Hardrada of Norway and had invaded northern England. As

Harold gathered his men and rushed north, the Saxon army of the north, led by the Earl of Northumbria, were defeated on 20 September at Fulford Gate. Five days later Harold surprised and annihilated the Norwegian invaders, slaying Tostig and Harald in the process, at Stamford Bridge.

WILLIAM'S INVASION

Back in France, William had been kept in Normandy by contrary winds. It was only on 12 September that his armada could sail to St Valéry on the Somme River from where he intended to invade England. It was only a short day's sailing across the Channel to England from this small port. The winds proved fickle and it was not until 27 September that a southerly wind allowed William's fleet to set sail northwards. He made landfall at Pevensey Bay the following morning and immediately set about gathering supplies, erecting his wooden forts (portable ones brought from Normandy in sections) and plundering the surrounding countryside for intelligence, food and fodder for his horses.

News that William had finally landed reached Harold at York on 1 October amidst celebrations following Stamford Bridge. Harold rushed south picking up the fyrd and other troops along the way back to London. He left the capital on 11 October heading south with an army of 6000–7000 troops. Many of his men rode to the battle on horses but would fight on foot. It was late in the afternoon on 13 October that Harold reached Senlac Ridge, a location that he had, during the summer's idleness, chosen as a possible battleground. His choice was based on his experience fighting the Welsh (1064) and his familiarity with the Hastings region.

Senlac was a gently sloped ridge with a marsh area to the south around the Asten brook with its western and eastern flanks protected by deep ravines covered by thick brushwood. An even steeper ridge protected the northern side and would thus prevent the Normans attacking Harold's army in the rear. William was rapidly informed about

Harold's movement and the arrival of his army. As the Saxons had arrived late in the day they would opt to rest and then make a lightning attack in the morning. But William would himself make the first move. His men were roused little after five in the morning and by 6.00 a.m. the Normans were marching northwards to face Harold's host. Before they set off William spoke to them telling them, 'You fight not merely for victory but also for survival'.

William's claim may seem melodramatic but it was the naked truth: if they failed to defeat the Saxons on hostile English soil then they would probably not escape home to Normandy alive. William divided his army into three divisions that marched off with the Bretons as the vanguard, followed by the Franco-Flemish troops and then finally William leading his own Normans. William had chosen as the assembly point the Blackhorse Hill, on the Hastings to London road, where the Bretons arrived by 7.30 a.m. Here, out of sight of the Saxons, William left his baggage train and ordered his men to put on their chain-mail hauberk armour which they had slung across the back of their horses. Unfortunately William put his hauberk on back-to-front, viewed by his superstitious men as a bad omen, but one that the cynical William simply laughed off. The Norman army marched north to take up position opposite the Saxons.

DISPOSITIONS

William remained on a small knoll out of the way under the Papal banner and his own Norman leopard standards. From this position he could give orders and had a good view of the battlefield. He could observe how the Bretons under Count Alan of Brittany followed the Asten brook to take up position opposite Harold's right flank. On William's left, Count Eustace of Boulogne led his French and Flemish mercenaries to the bottom of Senlac Ridge facing the Saxon left. In the middle now stood the largest and most formidable of the divisions: William's own Normans with auxiliaries from Anjou and Main. The archers and crossbowmen were

NORMAN KNIGHT

During the eleventh century, Norman horsemen dominated five military theatres: England, northern France, southern Italy, Sicily and the Holy Land. Their body armour, called a hauberk by this time, was mail and made in one piece. Most hauberks reached to the knees and were divided down the front and back by slits that allowed greater freedom of movement and comfort. Other defensive equipment included the kite shield and helmet. A long lance was the chief weapon of the Norman horseman, while a sword could be used for close combat.

at the front, then came the more heavily armed infantry and finally William's mounted men-at-arms.

For his part, Harold had been aware that the invaders were on the move since 8.00 a.m. when his scouts reported that the Normans had left Blackhorse Hill. If the weather had been wetter, forcing William to postpone his attack for a few crucial hours, Harold might have had time to erect proper defences atop Senlac Ridge but there was no rain and the ground was firm. Harold's army was roused and began to deploy along the ridge in a shield wall that stretched for 549m (600 yards) from the Asten brook to the junction of the roads to Hastings and Seddlescombe. The Saxon phalanx was 10 ranks deep with 0.6m (2ft) of frontage for each of his warriors meaning that he had about 6300 men under his command. As William had placed his strongest division in the centre, so Harold followed suit, placing his

ENGLISH SHIELD WALL, mid-eleventh century. The troops are mainly spearmen, although some hold axes and swords. The formation depended upon the mutual support of the men within it for its strength.

A ROMANTIC PORTRAYAL of William the Conqueror from a nineteenth-century illustration. Born an illegitimate son of the Duke Robert of Normandy, he became one of the greatest military leaders in history, fighting off rebels in his own duchy and conquering Maine, parts of Brittany and England.

more experienced huscarls in the centre. He placed his lighter armed and armoured men of the fyrd on the flanks, reinforced by a line of sharpened wooden stakes in front.

THE BATTLE BEGINS

The 14 October, the Feast of St Calixtus, dawned with brightening skies, a thin cloud cover and no indication of rain. Aged 44, Harold faced the 38-year-old William. They were both gifted and experienced commanders in their prime leading two of the best armies in western Europe, whose morale was superb: the Normans because of the prospect of conquest and loot, the Saxons because of the need to defend their homeland and their recent spectacular victory at Stamford Bridge. The Normans, who would have to make the first move, were 137m (150 yards) from, and 15.24m (50ft) below, the Saxon shield wall. The Bretons were the least experienced of William's troops and the weak link in his army. Harold's equivalent were the fyrd and he trusted his shield wall to hold back the onrush of Norman cavalry – it was the first time a predominantly cavalry army was fighting infantry in this fashion. The outcome would decide the nature of medieval warfare thereafter.

Sharp trumpet blasts at 9.00 a.m. announced the beginning of the battle as William's three divisions advanced up the slope of Senlac Ridge. The archers at the front showered the Saxons with arrows but to little effect – these either overshot their intended target or got lodged in the shield wall. The Saxon response with javelins, spears and axes proved far more effective against the onrushing Normans. As they had the gentler slope, the jittery Bretons were the first to smash into the shield wall and be repelled by the fierce resistance of the Saxons. Unnerved by this and the failure of the archers' fire to make any impact upon the shield wall, the

Bretons retreated by 10–10.30 a.m. The retreat turned into a rout when the undisciplined fyrd militia left the safety of the shield wall to purse the fleeing Bretons.

WILLIAM'S ATTACK

From his vantage point, William saw what was happening and with a curse he gathered part of the advancing Norman cavalry to assist the hard-pressed Bretons. Riding into the fyrd with a charge of armoured knights, the Saxons were taken by surprise and, as lightly armoured infantry on open ground, they were cut down to the last man. William's timely and ferocious cavalry charge had saved his army from disaster. Undoubtedly morale, especially among the defeated Bretons, was low. William recalled his other two divisions, halted for half an hour to regroup for another attack. This time the advance would be slower and more deliberate with the cavalry

THE MOST FEARSOME military tactic of the Middle Ages was the cavalry charge, as demonstrated here by Norman horse. At a time when success in battle often depended more on forcing one's enemies to flee the battlefield than on actually killing them, resisting such a charge depended on the discipline of lower-class infantry troops.

at the helm supported by archers and infantry following behind. William, taking personal charge, began the second attack at 11.00 a.m. As the ground was slippery from the previous attack and littered with dead men and horses, progress was slow and hesitant.

Waves of attacks were launched against the shield wall for two hours. The Normans managed to make a few, small holes in the line but Harold and his commanders, including his brothers Gyrth (Earl of East Anglia) and Leofwine (Earl of Kent), steadied their men, plugged the gaps and showered the enemy with missiles. Harold's Fighting Man standard and the Dragon Pennant of Wessex had been placed at the centre of the Saxon lines to encourage the defenders.

NEAR-ROUT

Finally, by 1.00 p.m., even the tough Flemish and French troops had had enough, they broke and began to flee from the ridge. Their commander Eustace grabbed the Papal standard, rallied his fleeing men and admonished them to return to the fight. William had already lost his Spanish charger and was fighting on foot when a rumour reached him that he was dead. Eustace gave the Duke a horse to mount and show himself to his men. William tore off his helmet so that his troops could recognize him and shouted: 'Look at me well. I am still alive and by the grace of God shall yet prove victor!' In reality William was losing the battle and he stared defeat in the face. Should the Saxons hold their line indefinitely then he would have been forced to retreat back to Hastings and return across the English Channel.

At 2.00 p.m. William called his men and returned them to his own lines below the ridge to regroup, rest and feed his hungry men. Harold used this respite to shorten his thinning line since Saxon losses, whatever the Normans may have thought, had been considerable and Harold was worried that he would run out of men to plug the ever-rising number of holes in the line. But at least his men were more rested than the Normans who faced an ever more debris-ridden and cluttered slope as they prepared for a renewed attack.

Having lost a quarter of his army, or around 1800–1900 men, in five hours of almost continuous fighting, as well as a horrendous number of horses, cut down by the axe-wielding Saxons, William saw that many of his men-at-arms were now fighting on foot. He decided that the whole army would attack in a single formation of all arms combined.

The third and final attack saw the entire army advance with archers at the back, from around 3.00 p.m., at a slow pace. It took the Normans an agonizing half-hour to reach the Saxon line. William had ordered the archers to shoot as high as possible while the infantry, dismounted knights and still-mounted cavalry gave their utmost in attacking the shield wall. Finally the shield wall began to waver, break in places and then come apart under the Norman onslaught. Once a

hole had been created in wall the Norman cavalry poured through and, with their lances, swords and spears, tore at the soft underbelly of the Saxon army. After 4.00 p.m. the breach became unstoppable and the fighting degenerated into group actions and hand-to-hand combat. This fighting went on until 5.30 p.m. with undiminished ferocity as men fought for their lives. Then the fyrd began to retreat, fleeing into the woods while the huscarls fought on until they were overwhelmed and killed. A large group rallied around Harold's standard as William joined his men on the ridge and had his third and final horse killed under him. Harold led his men with customary tenacity and courage, setting a personal example for his huscarls. But there were not enough of them to fight back the Normans. Gyrth and Leofwin, leading their own huscarls, were killed.

The final straw was the death of Harold himself. He was cut down by the Normans leading his few remaining huscarls. As darkness closed in on the battlefield, small groups of Saxons continued fighting until they could slip away into the surrounding countryside. They rallied and ambushed the pursuing Normans at Oakwood Gill, a small stream north of Senlac Ridge, and managed to cut down Eustace of Boulogne. That was small consolation for the death of Harold.

AFTERMATH

Both sides had lost more than 2000 men, the Normans well over a third of their army. For William, it was a triumph against the odds that paved the way for him being crowned as King of England on 25 December 1066. The Saxons would continue to resist their Norman invader for decades after their defeat at Hastings, but were eventually defeated.

SAXON HUSCARL

The Huscarls were an oath-sworn bodyguard of the Anglo-Danish aristocracy, which ruled England prior to the Norman Conquest of 1066. This man wields a long-handled axe which could decapitate a horse. He has slung his kite-shaped shield on his back to allow him a double-handed grip for extra weight in the blow.

HASTINGS

1 Harold Godwinson orders his troops into a shield wall along the top of Senlac Hill, with his heavier Huscarls positioned in the centre.

2 [text obscured] ... with arrow and ... The retreating English ... from the battlefield, giving the Norman victory.

3 The Breton infantry on the flank retreat and the English fyrd break their shield wall to chase them from the battlefield. However, under William's command, the Norman cavalry cut down the pursuing Saxon infantry.

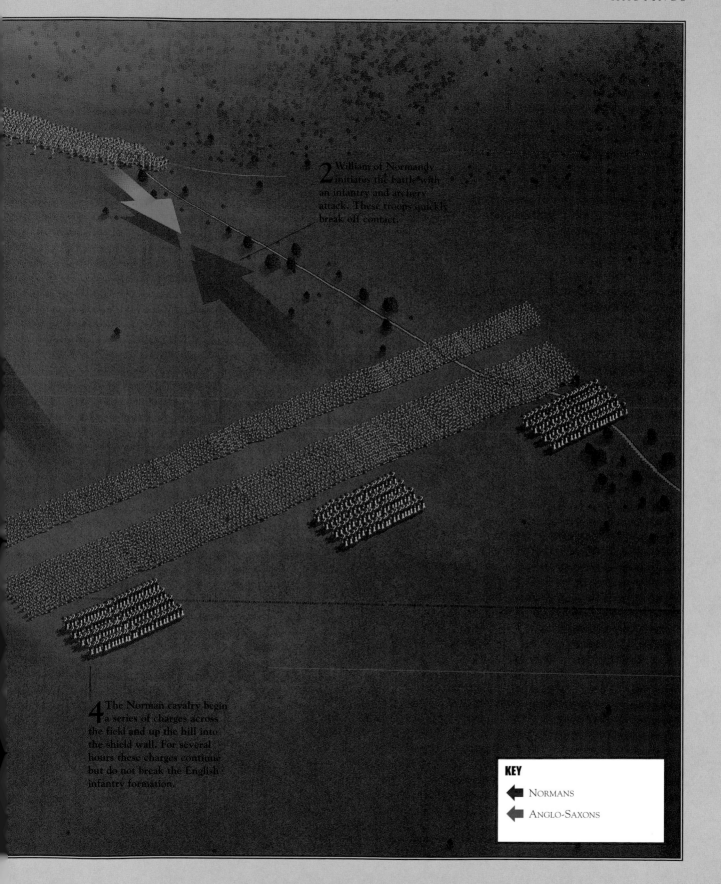

2 William of Normandy initiates the battle with an infantry and archery attack. These troops quickly break off contact.

4 The Norman cavalry begin a series of charges across the field and up the hill into the shield wall. For several hours these charges continue but do not break the English infantry formation.

KEY

◀ NORMANS

◀ ANGLO-SAXONS

HATTIN 1187

Hattin was a great victory for Saladin, who used his faster, lighter forces to great effect. He was assisted to a great extent by his enemy King Guy, who chose to march heavily armoured troops through a waterless region at the hottest time of the year.

The Crusades pitted two very different military systems against each another. On the Christian side, the arm of decision was the heavily armoured cavalry, which could smash an enemy formation and ride down the broken remains – assuming it made contact. This knightly host was supported by infantry – spearmen and crossbowmen – who were not greatly valued by their social betters among the cavalry. The fighting style of the Christians tended to be undisciplined and badly coordinated, though aggressive and courageous.

Against this powerful but clumsy blunt instrument was ranged the lighter, more mobile and (usually) highly-trained Muslim military system, which contained lighter troops for the most part but was better disciplined and organized than its enemy. Its cavalry component was largely made up of mail-armoured askari from Egypt and

HATTIN FACTS

Who: Crusader forces numbering around 32,000 under King Guy of Jerusalem (reigned 1186–92), versus a Seljuk Turkish army of 50,000 under Saladin (1138–93).

What: Harried to exhaustion by the more manoeuvrable Turks, the Crusaders were surrounded and eventually overwhelmed.

Where: The Horns of Hattin, Galilee.

When: June 1187.

Why: The Crusader force was marching to relieve a fortress and was intercepted by Saladin's army.

Outcome: The Crusader force was virtually annihilated.

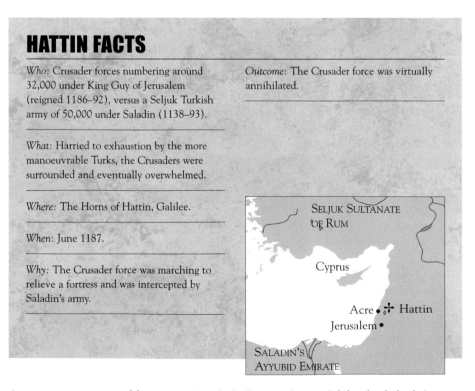

A ROMANTICIZED VERSION of the remaining Crusader leaders surrendering to Saladin after the battle (painting by S. Tahssin). Shortly after this the man who broke the truce, Reynald de Chatillon, and all the surviving Knights Templar and Hospitaller, were executed by Saladin.

THE HORNS OF HATTIN IN Galilee today. This photograph shows a rough, rocky terrain that would have been hard going for the Crusader heavy cavalry but which would not have hindered the lighter Muslim horse archers.

As the Turcopoles were driven off or destroyed, the Crusader column had no counter to the attacks of the Saracen skirmishers, except to keep the valuable knights and their horses inside a protective screen of infantry. Whilst still about 2km (1.25 miles) short of the intended battle area, the column was halted and preparations made to camp. There was no water available but the troops were too tired to go on. Between the heat and the constant attacks of the skirmishers the powerful column had been nibbled to death. The rearguard in particular was in a terrible state.

Having camped overnight without water, the Crusader army was in a desperate plight the following day. There was no possibility of going back, not through that wasteland with mounted skirmishers dogging every step. The objective lay just a couple of kilometres ahead, and obtaining water was now a critical requirement. The only option was to go on.

The Crusader force gathered its resolve and set off early in the morning, driving onwards to try to reach the nearest source of water, which lay in the village of Marescallia. The exhausted troops were halted well short of their objective by Muslim forces, who had been resupplied by camel trains during the night and were in good shape to fight.

THE BATTLE OPENS

In accordance with the ancient principle of not giving battle until you have already won, Saladin had allowed his enemy to exhaust himself, cut off his own retreat and then stumble to a disorganized halt in the face of relatively light opposition. And still Saladin did not commit to a decisive charge. He was a clever and patient man, who did not need dramatic results to know he had won. He would settle for quietly getting what he wanted at a lower price and always had an eye to the long-term strategic situation.

Saladin's forces advanced in a crescent formation, but stopped short of contact. Instead they poured arrows into the exhausted and disordered Crusader force. This placed the Crusaders in a terrible dilemma. The Crusaders could unleash their famous cavalry charge which, weakened as it was, still represented a tremendous amount of striking power. However, it was likely that the charge would hit only empty air as the Saracens faded away, shooting all the time. Alternatively the Crusaders could do nothing, and be steadily shot down. All the while their strength was being depleted by heat and thirst, and by arrows shot deliberately at the knights' horses to rob the Crusaders of their main striking power.

It was all too much for the hard-pressed infantry. Desperately thirsty, with the wasteland to their backs and thoroughly sick of being little more than walking archery butts, they tried to push on to the Sea of Galilee, which was visible not far away. The disorganized mob that had been the Crusader infantry was unable to break through to the shores of the sea, and was deflected by elements of the Muslim force. The infantry took refuge on the slopes of the easternmost of two hills nearby, known as the Horns of Hattin. There they stayed, refusing or ignoring orders, pleas and demands to rejoin the battle. Most were massacred after the battle proper. The rest were sold as slaves by their captors.

THE KNIGHTS ATTACK

There was no option now but to attack and try to break through the Muslim force. Raymond, with about 200 knights of the vanguard, was ordered forward and made his gallant, if ultimately doomed, run at the enemy.

As had happened many times before, the Saracens declined to receive the Crusader charge, but melted out of the way, shooting at the knights from flanks and rear as they passed. Raymond was wounded in three places and had been unable to make contact with the enemy. His weakened horses were blown and there was no prospect of achieving anything but a fairly inglorious death, so Raymond led what was left of his force out of the deathtrap and headed for Tyre. Saladin seemed content to let him go.

The remainder of the Crusader knights also launched charges at the Saracen force. The result was much the same; the highly mobile Muslim force evaded the clumsy charges and shot down the knights and their horses, closing in to cut off small contingents that could then be overwhelmed.

Some of the knights, perhaps 300 in all, were able to

break free and reach Acre. The remainder were gradually driven onto the western Horn of Hattin where they were no better off than the infantry on the eastern one. King Guy had his tent pitched on the hill, marking the centre of the defensive position.

Saladin had already won, but the cornered Crusaders might still inflict heavy casualties on his force if he decided to charge in and seek a dramatic ending. Instead he was content to bottle the Crusaders up on their waterless refuge and slowly destroy them with archery.

The Crusaders defended the area around the king's tent for as long as they were able, launching weak and abortive counter-attacks that had no chance of success. Even when the Saracens set fire to the brush, tormenting the thirsty Crusaders with smoke on top of all their other miseries, the knights held out as best they could.

Finally, though their strength gave out and the king's tent was overrun. The survivors surrendered, among them King Guy, Reynald and Gerard as well as about 150 knights. The Saracens took so many prisoners that they could not find enough rope to secure them all.

MUSLIM SOLDIERS set upon a fallen Crusader cavalryman. Once a horseman had been brought down from his mount, his opponents generally had the advantage.

VICTORY FOR SALADIN

Saladin had his most implacable enemies executed: Reynald and every Knights Templar or Hospitaller he could find. He also massacred the surviving Turcopoles, who were seen as traitors by their countrymen. Thousands of Crusader soldiers were sold into slavery, causing such a glut in the market that the price dropped considerably. Saladin did show mercy, however. King Guy was spared, as was Raymond's wife. She had to surrender the castle, but was allowed to depart unharmed. Guy was freed upon payment of what was literally a king's ransom. Saladin's victory at Hattin was partly due to failures of logistics, planning and common sense among the Crusaders, though it also owed a lot to the patience and cunning of Saladin himself. One of the great military axioms says 'do not interrupt the enemy while he is making a mistake' and Saladin was clever enough to let his foes hang themselves before he even considered joining battle. When he did fight it was with good tactics and sound logistics – a potent combination on any battlefield.

AFTERMATH

Hattin was the beginning of the end for the Crusaders. More Crusades would be launched and some successes would be scored, but the days of the great Crusader kingdoms were more or less over. Some 30 Crusader castles fell within the year, and Jerusalem surrendered to Saladin. This was in addition to the 11 cities handed over to Saladin's control as the ransom for King Guy.

The struggles for the Holy Land would go on, of course, but it was at Hattin that the Crusaders threw away all their advantages, and perhaps their chances of winning in the long term.

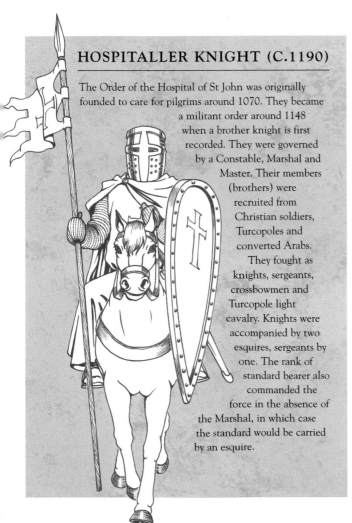

HOSPITALLER KNIGHT (C.1190)

The Order of the Hospital of St John was originally founded to care for pilgrims around 1070. They became a militant order around 1148 when a brother knight is first recorded. They were governed by a Constable, Marshal and Master. Their members (brothers) were recruited from Christian soldiers, Turcopoles and converted Arabs. They fought as knights, sergeants, crossbowmen and Turcopole light cavalry. Knights were accompanied by two esquires, sergeants by one. The rank of standard bearer also commanded the force in the absence of the Marshal, in which case the standard would be carried by an esquire.

HATTIN

4 The heavy knights' charge fails to overcome the more flexible Arab skirmishing cavalry.

6 King Guy and the remaining knights halt at the western horn, which becomes the focal point of the Crusaders' last stand.

5 A portion of the Crusaders make a break for safety and manage to get back to Acre.

1 Despite being beset by skirmishing cavalry the Crusaders break camp and move off.

2 Desperately thirsty, the infantry break off from the line of march towards the Sea of Galilee. Arab cavalry quickly move to exploit the division of forces.

3 Like so many sheep, the Crusader infantry are herded onto the eastern horn. Those that are not cut down are rounded up to be sold into slavery.

KEY

⬅ SARACENS

⬅ CRUSADERS

TANNENBERG 1410

The decisive battle of Tannenberg, between the army of the Teutonic Knights and the Royal Army of Poland-Lithuania, brought to a halt the eastward expansion of the hitherto invincible military order and secured the independence of Poland-Lithuania.

Founded in Acre in 1190 to defend the Holy Land, the Teutonic Order was a military order of warrior-monks whose military and religious reputation could be equated with the Knights of St John or the Templars. But unlike their rivals the Teutonic Order moved the seat of their activities and crusades to the southern and eastern coasts of the Baltic. The neighbouring Poles, whose once united kingdom by this time had become divided into independent duchies, were under constant attack from these hostile pagans, although the Lithuanians, who had carved out a huge realm by conquering Mongol-occupied western Russia, had eventually become Christian and allies of the Poles.

But that still left the marauding and savage Prusy to be dealt with. Lacking resources or the willpower to deal with them, Prince Conrad of Mazovia, whose duchy

TANNENBERG FACTS

Who: The army of the Teutonic Order under their Grand Master Ulrich von Jungingen (d. 1410) fought the Royal Army of Poland-Lithuania under King Wladislaw II Jagiello (1350–1434).

What: The Royal Army of Poland-Lithuania, with Tartar (Mongol) and Russian auxiliaries, annihilated the more experienced and heavily armed Teutonic army.

Where: On a shallow grass plain between the East Prussian (Mazurian) villages of Tannenberg and Grünwald.

When: 15 July 1410.

Why: The Royal Army were caught by surprise when the whole Teutonic army bore

down on them before they were prepared but the Teutons squandered a great opportunity to secure a victory by not attacking first.

Outcome: The Polish-Lithuanian victory halted the Teutonic Order's eastward expansion and effectively broke its power.

THIS PAINTING BY POLISH MILITARY ARTIST *Wojciech von Kossak (1824–99) gives a taste of the bloody battle, with the Royal army in close combat with the Teutons – the screams of wounded men, the neighing of horses, the clank of armour; dust, heat, and sudden death.*

was most exposed to Prusy attacks, in 1230 invited the Teutonic Order to crush the Prusy. The Order was only too glad to oblige and a decade later the Prusy threat had been eliminated leaving only pockets of resistance. Conrad quickly regretted ever having invited these rapacious and acquisitive Germans into territories that Poland viewed as vassal states.

EASTWARD EXPANSION

By 1283 the Order controlled both western and eastern Pruthenia or Prussia including the vitally important seaport city of Danzig (now Gdansk) – Poland's only port and point of contact with the West. As if this was not bad enough the Teutonic Order merged with the Order of the Sword Brethren – it too composed of German warrior-monks – that had conquered the Baltic states including the great seaport of Riga. The Order was now the dominant military and political power in the region and a growing threat to its neighbours especially as its huge state was backed by the region's best army and cavalry force.

The Poles, Lithuanians and the Novgorod Russians were equally threatened by the Order. Through a victory over the Sword Brethren in 1242 at Lake Peipus, Novgorod had been saved. It was Poland's turn next. The Order, meanwhile, had not only conquered Prussia but during the period 1310–50 encouraged German colonists to establish 1400 villages in the territory. Clearly the Order intended not only to conquer but colonise Poland and Lithuania as well despite both nations being loyal Christians.

In the face of an overwhelming threat Poland was finally, in 1320, re-united under King Wladislaw I (1320–33). Civil

LITHUANIAN INFANTRYMAN of the fifteenth century were armed in a variety of ways, including long-handled axes (as here), conical, Norse-style helmets and chainmail. This was a consequence of Lithuania's geographical location, which reflected a mixture of Nordic and Russian military and cultural influences.

THIS DRAMATIC BATTLE SCENE shows Grand Duke Jagiello supposedly tearing the standard from a Teutonic Knight, signalling the order's defeat.

war and chaos threatened when he left no male heirs, Poland being ruled by his daughter Queen Jadwiga. She, however, proved a shrewd and able ruler in her own right and she offered her hand in marriage – in order to unite Poland and Lithuania – to the much older Lithuanian Grand Duke Jagiello (1350–1434) who had only recently been christened, appropriately enough, Wladislaw.

Poland had acquired a powerful ally in their quest to crush the Order and regain control over Danzig and Prussia. Lithuania had a formidable army in its own right that had defeated the Mongols and emulated their superlative tactics, equipment and horsemanship of the steppes' lightning war. In 1386 Jadwiga married Jagiello and the Royal Commonwealth of Poland-Lithuania was founded. When the Order sought to wrest the Lithuanian province of Samogitia from the Grand Duke, Poland was ruled by Jagiello. War was now inevitable but shrewdly Jagiello wanted his enemy to make the first move.

THE OPPOSING ARMIES

Fighting, let alone defeating the Order, was no easy proposition for Jagiello since the Order's army had been victorious ever since its appearance in the region in 1230. Its heavy cavalry of men-at-arms clad in white surcoats with black crosses, numbering some 2000–3000 men, were probably the best in Europe and formed the superlative core of an outstanding military machine. Superbly disciplined, mounted, equipped, trained and experienced, the Teutonic Knights had no equals in Europe let alone the east Baltic region. But with the technological progress of the fourteenth century, the Order had to supplement its knights with mercenaries and specialists such as English longbowmen, Genoese crossbowmen, German and Swiss infantry and French artillery. All in all the army of the Order was a dangerous and formidable foe.

By contrast the Poles and Lithuanians were far weaker and with less reason to be confident of a victory if faced with the grim-faced German warrior-monks. The Poles had a conventional European-style medieval army of no particular distinction or reputation as yet. As in France the Polish infantry was made up of reluctant, poorly disciplined and motivated peasant conscripts who would rather be working on their farms than fighting their proud and uncaring Lord's wars. In the face of the superior Teutonic infantry they would either fight with customary Polish bravery or, if the mood took them, simply run away at the first enemy charge. The cavalry, mainly composed of Poland's proud and insanely brave nobility, were well mounted, equipped and motivated. While they were more than a match, man-for-man, to the Teutons, they lacked the warrior-monks' experience and discipline.

MEDIEVAL ARMOUR SUITS *were most often made of chain links or metal scales. Chain armour (favoured in western Europe) consisted of thousands of round metal rings, the ring ends welded or riveted together. Scale armour (favoured in Eastern Europe and Byzantium) was made of a large number of metallic scales attached to each other by wire or leather laces.*

By contrast the Lithuanian host was more Asiatic than European in appearance, equipment and tactics as they had fought for centuries against the Mongol occupiers of Russia. As a consequence they placed great reliance upon skirmishing, manoeuvring and mobility with light and medium cavalry forces rather than a head-on collision with heavy cavalry and massed infantry. If these warriors faced the

IN THIS PAINTING *by Jan Matejko (1838–93), the Polish-Lithuanian army is at the point of crushing the reeling and bleeding troops of the order, with a triumphant Jagiello in the centre of the action.*

TEUTONIC KNIGHT

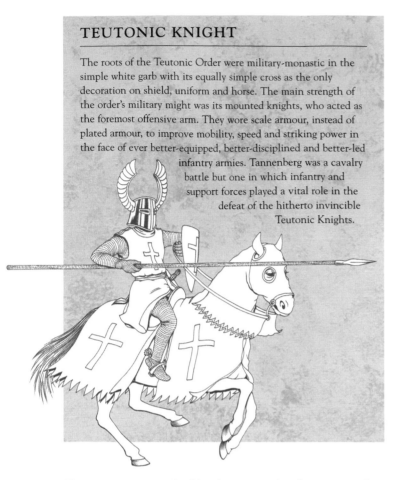

The roots of the Teutonic Order were military-monastic in the simple white garb with its equally simple cross as the only decoration on shield, uniform and horse. The main strength of the order's military might was its mounted knights, who acted as the foremost offensive arm. They wore scale armour, instead of plated armour, to improve mobility, speed and striking power in the face of ever better-equipped, better-disciplined and better-led infantry armies. Tannenberg was a cavalry battle but one in which infantry and support forces played a vital role in the defeat of the hitherto invincible Teutonic Knights.

Teutons in open pitched battle in a confined space – as they were to do at Tannenberg – it was dubious whether they would be able to make a stand.

THE CAMPAIGN

In December 1409 during a meeting at Brest-Litovsk Jagiello, the Polish commanders and his cousin, Duke Witold, the Viceroy of Lithuania, agreed to combine their armies at a rendezvous on the Vistula, called Czerwinsk, where it was safe to cross the river barrier. It was safe from there to invade Prussia and hopefully defeat the Order on home ground. Meanwhile Jagiello secured the neutrality of the Order's Livonian knights while the friendly King of Hungary, who had signed an alliance with the Order, assured the Poles that he would not support his newfound allies. Thus the Commonwealth had no reason to fear a diversionary attack on their extensive southern and northeastern frontiers leaving them free to concentrate their considerable military strength against the Teutons.

To keep the Order's army (dispersed along the frontier) on its toes, Jagiello ordered diversionary offensives against Pomerania and Memel. In the meantime, using a 600m (550 yard) long pontoon bridge across the Vistula, the Poles and

Lithuanians had combined at the Czerwinsk bridgehead by 30 June. They marched northward on 2 July. Ulrich von Jungingen, the Grand Master of the Teutonic Order, had failed to concentrate his army since he underestimated his enemy in general and his technical expertise – he could not believe the 'primitive' Poles and Lithuanians capable of building pontoon bridges! His racial arrogance was to cost him his life and the existence and reputation of his army as well. In a mere eight days the Royal Army had covered 90km (82 miles) – a phenomenal rate of advance for a medieval army – crossing the Prussian frontier already on 2 July 1410. Ulrich was caught by surprise again and was forced to concentrate his scattered army at Kurzetnik where, on 3 July, Jagiello's army joined him. The two armies were now poised for battle.

DISPOSITIONS

Ulrich built a series of bridges across the Drweça river in order for his army to cross over to its eastern bank where the battlefield formed a rough triangle between three small Prussian villages – Tannenberg, Grünwald and Ludwigsdorf. In this partly wooded and rough terrain visibility could have been better. The battlefield was shaped like a shallow soup plate measuring 3km (1.9 miles) in diameter.

Jagiello's combined army numbered 10,000–20,000 infantry and as many as 40,000 cavalry (including Tartar auxiliaries) while the Grand Master had 21,000 cavalry and a mere 6000 infantry. The Royal Army's camp was situated 7.2km (4.5 miles) east of Grünwald at Lake Lubien while the Order's army had moved across the river into the field. At dawn on 15 July a Polish knight and scout, Hanko, entered the camp and informed Jagiello that the enemy was already drawn up for battle. Ulrich had caught the enemy – only forming up slowly – by surprise and should have, in hindsight, attacked immediately with all force and determination. Instead Ulrich ordered his men to dig ditches and form the army in two lines. His decision was the more faulty since here was open ground with good visibility well suited for a massed cavalry attack up to the slopes of the ridge that led to Lake Lubien and the Royal army's camp.

THE BATTLE

But nothing happened since Ulrich wanted the enemy to make the first move and they – primarily the cautious and shrewd Jagiello – were reluctant to act. As the morning hours wore on and his men grew impatient, Ulrich decided to goad the 'cowardly' Poles and Lithuanians into action. He sent Duke Kazimir of Stettin (Szczeczin) whose shield bore the Black Eagle on a gold background (symbol of the Holy Roman Emperor) and the Imperial Herald to rebuke Jagiello for not fighting like a man. Jagiello, hoping to negotiate a peaceful settlement, received the two knights politely but was rudely told that his army should come out to fight like men on the

IN THIS ROMANTICIZED nineteenth-century oil painting by the Polish artist Maksymiljan Piotrowski (1813–75), the Polish-Lithuanians, led by their venerable-looking king, Wladislaw II, prepare for battle on 15 July 1410.

field of battle. Jagiello gave as good as he got, telling the two arrogant knights that they would regret their insults in a few hours and they, like the Grand Master, would get more than they had bargained for. He gave a signal for Witold to commence the battle.

The Poles advanced in good order on the left while the Lithuanians, Russians and Tartars could not control themselves and threw themselves at the Germans who buckled under the onslaught. The Teutonic knights counter-attacked, slaying the enemy, and the Lithuanian army began to falter and retreat as the Tartars (either fleeing or executing a feigned retreat) moved out of range. Only Witold's central regiments held the line and Witold was forced, in person, to beg his cousin to save his flank.

Jagiello sent his last remaining reserves that managed to stem the Teutonic advance but as the dust settled Ulrich noticed how exposed the Polish King was on a small knoll on the battlefield, and sent a small force to either kill or capture Jagiello. The assassination attempt failed since some alert Polish knights saw what was happening and moved to intercept the Teutons. Witold used this time to rally his men who turned around and rode back to the centre of the battlefield. It was the Teutons' turn to be caught unawares as Tartar arrows, Russian battleaxes and Lithuanian swords cut at

them. The Poles, having held their line, forced the Order's knights back and surrounded them. Ulrich, stubborn, proud yet brave, chose like his men to stand and fight where they stood and as consequence they were cut down. Few remained alive when the battle finally ended, at 7.00 p.m., at the village of Grünwald. Some 14,000 of the Order's knights and soldiers had been taken prisoner while the rest (18,000) lay strewn dead or dying on the dusty battlefield.

AFTERMATH

Instead of marching on the Teutonic Order's capital of Marienburg to the west, the Polish-Lithuanian army – utterly exhausted – remained on the battlefield to divide the loot, rest and recuperate. When it was ready to march on Marienburg – held by Count Heinrich von Plauen and 3000 troops – it was too late. This immense fortress complex with stone walls 8.2m (27ft) high and 2.1m (7ft) thick and ample supplies of food and water proved impregnable. Jagiello's victorious army arrived on 25 July but failed to make any headway during the two-month siege. The war would continue for years and the Order would eventually recover.

TANNENBERG

3 The Grand Master believes, with the enemy's right in disarray, that the time has come for a final push and sends a group of his toughest men to capture Jagiello. This lunge fails and with it any hope of a Teutonic victory.

6 The Order's army is completely wiped out with 18,000 dead littering the battlefield and the remaining 14,000 captured.

5 The battlefield is by afternoon a confusing tangle of struggling, dying and wounded men fighting each other in close combat where no mercy is given or expected. One by one the Teutonic Knights are overwhelmed.

1 After the Teutonic emissaries' taunts at first light, the Polish-Lithuanian army advance across the open fields towards the Teutonic lines. Their left flank attack with abandon but are stemmed by heavy Teutonic Knights.

2 Tartar cavalry make a controlled retreat in the hope of luring the knights into a trap but the right flank falls into disorder as retreat turns into rout.

4 The Tartars and Russians stop the retreat, re-form their lines and launch a devastating counter-attack, supported by the Lithuanians led by Grand Duke Jagiello.

KEY

POLISH/LITHUANIAN FORCES

TEUTONIC KNIGHTS

AGINCOURT 1415

The victory of Henry V's small, exhausted and starving army against a vast French host was the greatest triumph of the English longbow in the Hundred Years War between England and France. But despite the arrow-storm, the battle came to hand-to-hand combat, and was not the walkover for the English that it has often been portrayed as.

In 1413 Henry V, aged only 27, mounted the English throne with the ambition to wrest control of northern France. By early July 1415 Henry V had gathered in utmost secrecy a 12,000-strong army around Winchester while he collected suitable tonnage to ship his troops to France. On 11 August his army set sail from the south coast in 1500 ships, reaching the tip of the peninsula north of the Seine two days later. Early the next morning, 14 August, the English began to disembark. Fortunately for the English, the French Constable Charles d'Albret had expected Henry to land his army on the south side of the Seine as a prelude to a march on Paris.

Paris was not Henry's objective. Instead he had his eyes on the great fortified port city of Harfleur (Le Havre) located 1.6km (1 mile) up the Lézarde River, a tributary

AGINCOURT FACTS

Who: An English army of 6000 under King Henry V (1388–1422) defeated a French army of 36,000 under the command of Charles d'Albret, Constable of France (1369–1415).

What: Agincourt saw a small, well disciplined and entrenched English army defeat a far larger French army through massed archery.

Where: The battle took place near the Castle of Azincourt approximately half way between Calais and Abbeville in northern France.

When: Friday 25 October 1415.

Why: Henry sought to revive the English claim to the throne of France.

Outcome: Agincourt (Azincourt) was the greatest English victory of the Hundred Years War against France.

King Henry V makes a rallying speech to his troops on St Crispin's Day, inspiring his men for the desperate battle ahead. By nightfall the English had won one of the greatest victories of all time.

AT AGINCOURT, KING HENRY V ordered that every archer should cut himself a stake to provide portable protection against cavalry charges. This worked to great effect in defeating the French.

undermine the walls and English artillery fired into the city both day and night. A month later and both sides were suffering from the effects of dysentery, the 'bloody flux' as it was called, and an acute shortage of food. Henry met Gaucourt on 17 September but the stubborn French nobleman, impervious to Henry's threats and flattery alike, refused to accept terms for surrender despite having lost a third of his garrison during the five-week siege.

Gaucourt's only hope was that the Dauphin, Prince Louis de Guienne, would come to his relief. Guienne – a fat, indolent, foppish 18-year-old – was hardly the man to risk leading a relief force to aid the hard-pressed garrison of Harfleur. Fearing an English assault and subsequent massacre, the populace beseeched Gaucourt to capitulate, which he did on 22 September. It was sweet revenge for Henry who had been left fuming five days earlier.

THE MARCH TO CALAIS

Henry's councillors, including Clarence, urged the King to return in triumph to England and leave France to its civil wars and strife. Henry refused, so Clarence took his own advice and returned home in a huff, leaving the King to plan

AN ENGLISH FOOTSOLDIER takes a French nobleman captive at the Battle of Agincourt in 1415. This image symbolizes the superiority that infantrymen could exercise over their social betters.

of the Seine, protected by tidal salt marshes and a lake. Harfleur was held by 400 knights under the command of the experienced and courageous Raoul de Gaucourt.

By 19 August the English had invested Harfleur from all sides, with the Duke of Clarence in the east blocking access and relief (if it ever came) from Rouen while Henry was camped on the port's western side. Henry ordered siege lines to be erected while Clarence's Welsh miners dug tunnels to the next stage of his campaign. Harfleur was a small prize for such a huge effort and Henry was hardly a man to rest on his laurels. He wanted to lure the French into fighting a pitched battle and defeat them decisively – anything less would be a failure.

Trusting in God and his men – 5000 archers and 900 men-at-arms – Henry left Harfleur on 6 October expecting to cover the 241km (150 miles) to Calais in a mere eight days. It would take a lot longer and prove a trying ordeal for his army – halved through the gruelling siege of Harfleur. The French, ably led by d'Albret, shadowed the movements of the English along the Somme and at the fording point of Blanche Taque 6000 French blocked their advance across the river, forcing Henry to continue along the southern bank of the river. On 15 October, when they should have reached Calais according to Henry's wildly optimistic calculations, the English slipped past Amiens. Both the troops and Henry's advisers began to wonder if they would ever get across the Somme.

Finally, four days later, having evaded the French army at Péronne by cutting across country and avoiding a bend in the Somme, the English reached Nesle where they found two undefended crossing points. They were safely across in a single day and could advance northwards on 21 October in good order, although in daily expectation of a French attack.

Wisely the French bided their time and d'Albret argued, like the Duke de Berry, that the French should avoid a pitched battle. Henry would have little to show for his efforts if he returned to Calais without having fought and won a battle. Harfleur could then be retaken. But the Royal Dukes (Orléans, Bourbon and Alençon) swept aside d'Albret's objections. They wanted to crush the English in the field and earn some much needed martial glory for themselves and France.

AGINCOURT

On 24 October came the news the English had dreaded but also looked forward to: the French army were drawn up in a flat plain between the villages of Azincourt, Tramecourt and Maisoncelle. Henry turned to his Welsh retainer, Dafyd Gam, asking him to estimate the vast French horde and Gam replied coolly: 'Sire. There are enough to kill, enough to capture and enough to run away.' In fact the French outnumbered the English six-to-one with 36,000 troops in all as they drew up a strong defensive position along the Calais road that cut across the Azincourt plain. Their flanks were protected by woodlands, their backs by open fields and only a small, shallow valley separated them from the puny English army.

During the night, Henry enforced total silence upon his men who were reduced to whispering. This eerie silence unnerved the French who expected it was an English ruse to escape their inevitable doom the following morning. They set up a picket line with fires at regular intervals along the road to prevent such an escape. Henry expected a night attack so he kept his men in battle order during much of the night. Henry did not sleep either as he made preparations for the coming battle and sent out scouts that returned with news that the ground resembled a muddy soup.

DISPOSITIONS

Henry decided to extend the English line between the woods and hedges surrounding the villages of Maisoncelle and Tramecourt. As the ground in front of the English line, fronted by a line of sharp stakes, had turned into a quagmire the French attack would be slowed down and prove a most welcoming target for his archers. Conditions were ideal and Henry placed the dismounted men-at-arms in the middle of his battle line and the archers on the flanks. The centre would be under Henry's personal command while the right was commanded by the Duke of York and the left by Thomas, Lord Camoys.

But Henry knew that his was a desperate and dangerous gamble. He had no reserves, there was no fall-back and he had nowhere close to escape to should he be defeated.

FRENCH KNIGHT

The large amount of warfare taking place in the fifteenth century led to some dramatic military technological changes. By 1400 cavalry began wearing a more solid breastplate made from a single piece of metal fashioned to cover the chest and sides. By the end of the century this had been joined to metallic plates covering the back, neck, legs, arms and feet, and was topped by a helmet with visor that fitted tightly around the head. Over this, the knight usually wore a heraldic surcoat. The knight would be armed with a lance and sword.

In this nineteenth-century illustration of Agincourt, it is the mounted knight that takes centre stage. Even today, it is widely (and erroneously) believed that medieval warfare was the exclusive province of the armoured nobleman.

Henry's single line could be outflanked should the French use part of their army to go around the woodlands and attack him in the rear. Even if the French made a frontal assault the English might be crushed by the sheer weight of the attack.

The French did, in fact, have a battle plan drawn up a few days before the battle. Boucicaut, Marshal of France, and Constable d'Albret would command the first French battle composed of 8000 dismounted men-at-arms, 4000 archers and 1500 crossbowmen. The main (centre) battle or division would be under Prince Charles d'Artois and Alençon with a similar number of troops, and flanked on the right and left by two wings of mounted men-at-arms under the respective command of Richemont and Bourbon.

There was a small rearguard of 1000 knights and a small force of 200 knights that would be sent around the woods to attack the English baggage train. In fact, the plan broke down even before it was implemented and instead of being preceded by a shower of arrows from their archers and crossbowmen, the French men-at-arms pushed them to the back of the formation. Instead, it was the flower of French chivalry that was to be sent forward to crush the small English army into the ground.

THE ENGLISH MEN-AT-ARMS *were always prepared to dismount to fight alongside the archers, who were their social inferiors. These longbowmen usually deployed on the flanks or in broken ground to give them protection against more heavily armed opponents should it come to hand-to-hand fighting.*

ST CRISPIN'S DAY

After a long, cold night of torrential rain the fields were even muddier as the sun rose on St Crispin's Day – Friday 25 October 1415. The English had spent the night in the open while the French had slept in tents and gorged themselves on wine and plentiful provisions. The French were sure that they would win an easy victory.

Hours passed as each side waited for the other to make the first move. The French had every reason to wait. With every passing hour their strength would increase and the English grow weaker. It was this realization that prompted a frustrated Henry to make the first move. It was a calculated gamble as he ordered his men to pull up their stakes, move forward in full view of the enemy, and erect a new line of stakes further in the gap between the woods, closer to the French, hoping to goad them into attacking. This narrowed the front considerably – a change that favoured the English and tore up the French plan. The French had originally thought of sending their cavalry to attack the flanks of the English line but now they were forced to make a frontal assault – exactly what they had hoped to avoid. The French realized that the ground sloped downwards toward the English line and the field tapered off into a funnel shape the closer they got to the stakes. Furthermore it was only now, quite belatedly, that the French – who had failed to send out scouts – realized the ground was dangerously muddy and soft.

Yet they were committed to a plan and stuck to it with disastrous results. The French chose to open the battle with

KING HENRY V, a portrait by Benjamin Burnell (1790–1828). One of England's great captains, Henry's real-life deeds at Agincourt and Harfleur would grant him a place in heroic legend, even if he had never been immortalized in Shakespeare's plays.

a cavalry charge that proved too puny – of 1200 knights on horse and only a third (420 men) actually attacked. Their noble colleagues on foot were quickly in trouble as their heavy armour pulled them into the mud below. As they floundered and sunk into the mud up to their knees Sir Thomas Erpingham (in command of the archers) gave the signal and then shouted the dreaded order – 'Now strike!'

Strong arms nocked arrows, pulled the bowstrings to their maximum extent and sought the greatest elevation before loosing off the first volley. Thousands of arrows whined through the air like a cloud before hitting the target or plopping into the muddy ground. Enough steel-tipped, armour-piercing bodkin arrows struck home to break up the French advance. Their effect upon the less protected horses was terrifying and master-less horses, bleeding and neighing wildly, ran back into the French lines trampling the dismounted knights into the mud.

Now an additional hindrance of dead and dying horses and men had been created for the dismounted knights to advance over. Despite the massed volleys, huge casualties and confusion, the dismounted knights pressed on with determination and heroism. They could see little because the arrows made it dangerous to put one's head up, even with an armoured helmet, as the English archers aimed straight at their visors. The knights were trapped inside their armour and their mobility, vision and breathing was dangerously restricted. Yet they continued advancing in their thousands.

HAND-TO-HAND COMBAT

The greatest honour of saving the English army from destruction at the hands of the French dismounted men-at-arms must go to the small number of English men-at-arms who halted and bloodied the French advance that reached right up to their lines. They were joined by squires, camp followers and an increasing number of archers who had run out of arrows, using any weapon at hand – axes, daggers and the mallets they had used to drive in their stakes – to cut, thrust, gouge and stab at the faltering French. Sheer numbers had crowded the French line preventing their knights from using their weapons effectively. The French were now so close that the archers could fire at them at point-blank range with devastating effect.

In this confused and grim hand-to-hand combat no quarter was given. As commoners, the English archers knew they would be slaughtered out of hand by the French since they had no value in terms of ransom. As a consequence the English were, quite literally, fighting for their lives and fought with even more ferocity than usual against the French

knights who might be captured alive and ransomed at a later date. This simple difference in psychology might explain the outcome of the battle.

For three gruesome, bloody hours the slaughter went on as the French dead piled up in heaps in front of the English lines. The English were growing weary with their deadly task. There was a last minute flurry among the French as the Duke of Brabant arrived in the afternoon. It came to nothing as Brabant was killed with his men. Alarmed by this, and fearing that the scores of French prisoners might take up arms again if there was another attack, Henry took no chances and broke all rules of chivalry by putting his prisoners to death where they stood.

AFTERMATH

There was no French rally or second attack as feared. Instead what remained of the French army fled the field of battle leaving thousand of dead, wounded and captured to the less-than-tender mercies of the English. The English had lost a mere 112 men, two-thirds archers, and had won the most miraculous of victories against all the odds and expectations. A month later Henry was back in England, his men were amply paid and England celebrated that wonderful Day of St Crispin while the traumatized French simply referred to Agincourt as 'that unfortunate day' (la malheureuse journée) for generations to come. The Hundred Years War was set to continue for another four decades.

AGINCOURT

6 The French mounted reserve launches a last futile charge, but is repulsed. Many French prisoners are executed in the confusion.

3 The cavalry routs back into the dismounted French second line, hurling it into confusion.

2 Flanking French cavalry units launch charges on the English archers, but are repelled by arrows and stakes.

KEY

← ENGLISH

← FRENCH

1 Heavily outnumbered English battle line of dismounted men-at-arms flanked by archers advances on the French.

4 The French main body struggles into position to attack the English but is overwhelmed, with many of its leaders subsequently taken prisoner.

5 An outflanking French force attacks the English baggage, killing its attendants and pillaging Henry's treasure.

97

THE AGE OF GUNPOWDER

Gunpowder and artillery revolutionized European warfare after its introduction during the fourteenth and fifteenth centuries and forced military commanders to develop fortresses and military tactics and strategies to deal with this new, devastatingly effective technology.

Having played a secondary role during the Middle Ages, the infantry regained its primary role on the battlefield with the rise of the musket. The musket was a great leveller, in that large numbers of men could be trained quickly to use it, putting an end to the dominance of the expensively-armed and armoured knight of the Middle Ages.

During the seventeenth and eighteenth centuries, muskets became less unwieldy, lighter and more accurate. By that time massed infantry armies made up of professional, regular troops fought each other in huge, packed series of lines, firing at each other with musket and canon shot at close range. In these deadly, close-range fire-fights just a handful of musket volleys could decide the outcome of a battle.

AS PART OF A REENACTMENT to commemorate the battle of Austerlitz, military history enthusiasts dressed as French soldiers shoot at the enemy, November 2003. This photograph suggests the deadly effectiveness of massed musket volleys, which could decimate an enemy column in a matter of minutes.

CONSTANTINOPLE

1453

The fall of Constantinople in 1453, its once-impregnable walls breached by Ottoman siege guns, brought to an end the Byzantine Empire and established the Ottoman Empire as the major threat to Christendom in the Mediterranean and Eastern Europe for the next two centuries.

The Byzantine Empire, once the bulwark of the Christian West against the Arabs and Turks, had been defeated by the Seljuk Turks at Manzikert in 1071 and in 1389 their descendants, the Ottoman Turks, defeated a Serb army at Kosovo Polje. By 1400 most of Asia Minor was in the hands of the Ottomans and it seemed only a matter of time before this once flourishing Imperial capital of a million inhabitants would fall to them. The irruption of Tamerlane (Timur Lenk) (1336–1405) into Asia Minor and his defeat of the Turks at Ankara in 1402 gave the hard-pressed Byzantines a short breathing space. In 1422 Sultan Murad II (ruled

CONSTANTINOPLE FACTS

Who: Sultan Mehmed II Fatih (1451–83) laid siege to Constantinople with an army of 120,000 men, opposed by a mere 10,000, Christian Greek and Italian defenders led by Emperor Constantine XI (1449–53).

What: Turks used, for the first time, massive siege artillery to blow a hole in the Theodosian Wall protecting the city.

Where: The city of Constantinople was the Imperial Byzantine capital (303–1453) located on a peninsula by the Bosporus, the Sea of Marmara and facing the Golden Horn in what is now Turkey.

When: 5 April–29 May 1453.

Why: The Ottoman Turks had expanded their empire in every direction and wished to

make Constantinople their capital and eliminate this Christian stronghold behind their lines.

Outcome: The city was taken with great bloodshed, and became the capital of the Ottoman Empire.

THE TURKS ENTERED CONSTANTINOPLE *on 29 May 1453. The Byzantine Emperor, Constantine XI, was killed. The sultan, Mehmed II, gave the city up to his troops to destroy and loot for three days.*

1421–51) laid siege to the city but Constantinople's defences repelled him and this gentlemanly scholar of a ruler left the Byzantines alone.

THE CANNON OF MEHMED II was cast in 1464 and used by the Turks to protect the Bosporus strait. The gun was divided into two parts for ease of transportation. It weighed 18.2 tonnes (18 tons) and was 5.25m (17ft) long.

MEHMED THE CONQUEROR

Unfortunately Murad died in 1451 leaving the throne to his arrogant and aggressive 19-year-old son, Mehmed (Muhammed) II, who for the next 30 years was to be a scourge upon his Muslim and Christian neighbours alike. Mehmed set out to prove himself an ardent Ghazi (holy warrior) by conquering Constantinople and all of Asia Minor and the Balkans.

The key to a successful siege of Constantinople was the ability to breach the massive 5.7km (3.5 mile) long Theodosian land wall with its moats, towers and triple layered lines of walls, walls that no army had been able to overcome in over a millennium! But Mehmed II had found a renegade Christian, Urban of Transylvania, willing to build a monster of a gun measuring 8.1m (26ft 8in) in length, with a calibre of 20.3cm (8in) that could lob a solid stone cannon ball weighing a ton over 1.6km (1 mile). Urban's monster gun was completed and ready for inspection by a most satisfied Mehmed in January 1453. It would take a crew of 700 to transport, load and handle the monster gun but it would prove most effective against the Theodosian Wall.

Unlike his father, Mehmed never honoured treaties made with the Christians. He occupied Byzantine lands

THIS DETAIL of a sixteenth-century fresco depicts Ottoman horse cavalry during the Siege of Constantinople.

across the Bosporus and cut the city's supplies of grain from Romania and southern Russia vital for its population. In five short months (April–August 1452) Mehmed had built a fort named Boghaz-Kesen (appropriately enough called the Throat Cutter) on the Bosporus whose sole purpose was to prevent shipping supplies reaching Constantinople. In November a Genoese vessel that ignored Mehmed's blockade was sunk with a single shot from one of the massive guns inside Boghaz-Kesen and its captain, Antonio Rizzo, was impaled while his men were put to death. Mehmed had warned the infidels not to try his severely limited patience and that the Byzantines were now at his mercy.

THE OPPOSED FORCES

The final nails in Constantinople's coffin came during the winter of 1452–3. Firstly, the Catholic West failed, as ever, to assist the Orthodox Christians against the common foe. Admittedly the Pope made frantic but ineffectual efforts to drum up support for a crusade against the deadly Turkish threat, but Genoa, which held the fortified suburb of Pera across the Golden Horn, refused to abandon her lucrative yet dubious 'neutrality'. Only Venice, Genoa's sworn enemy, with extensive and vulnerable Balkan colonies, proved willing and able to assist Constantinople.

No such mercenary spirits prevailed in the doomed city itself as Christians of Slav, Greek or Italian origin buried the hatchet in the face of the approaching, ruthless foe. Constantine XI who had only ascended the throne four years earlier proved not only a great orator but an inspired leader: he pointed out that they were all in the same boat, that they could not expect any mercy from Mehmed given the Genoese crew's gruesome fate and that the West might aid them after all.

These were no more than words of truth but of scant comfort to the outnumbered and now surrounded defenders with no more than 10,000 armed men. Mehmed's elite guard, the Janissaries, alone numbered 12,000 men and his whole army would be ten times that size (figures vary from 100,000 to 150,000 troops). What was far worse was that Mehmed had managed, through a massive effort, to create a real galley fleet – the first in Ottoman history – built and manned by renegade Balkan Christians. Its commander, the Grand Admiral of the Fleet (Kapudan Pasha), Suleyman Balthoghlu was a converted Bulgarian. To the consternation of the defenders this fleet entered the southern (Marmara) Sea in early March 1453. Now the Marmara Sea Wall was threatened as well, requiring a garrison from Constantine's tiny army.

THE SIEGE BEGINS

The first Ottoman troops, the vanguard, appeared beneath the Land Wall on 1 April and at a signal from Constantine

himself the gates were shut, the wooden bridges across the moat burnt and the walls manned. Constantinople was now clearly under siege and cut off from the rest of the world. Five days later Mehmed arrived with the main army and set up camp beneath the walls. The Byzantines were master fortifiers who had reinforced the massive Land Wall where it was weak, such as at Blachernae. They had left the Sea Walls along the Marmara and Golden Horn relatively weakly held, since intelligence reports told them Mehmed would concentrate upon the Land Wall.

On 9 April the Ottoman Fleet made a failed attempt to break through the boom that stretched across the Golden Horn from the Sea Wall to Pera while the army dealt with two outlying forts, Therapia and Studius. Both held out for two days. On Mehmed's express orders the defenders were impaled as a warning to Constantinople's defenders that the same gruesome fate awaited them. Mehmed's barbarity only made the besieged Christians more determined to fight to the death rather than capitulating to such a capricious and bloodthirsty tyrant. A third fort, on the island of Prikipo, saw the garrison burn themselves alive rather than surrender.

Three days later the Ottoman artillery began an unrelenting bombardment of the Land Wall that went on for six weeks. Urban's gun fired seven times a day but the damage wrought was easily repaired by the diligent defenders. By 18 April the wall across the Lycus valley – the weakest spot in the defences of the Land Wall – had

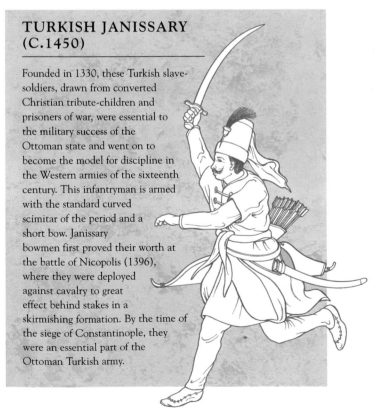

TURKISH JANISSARY (C.1450)

Founded in 1330, these Turkish slave-soldiers, drawn from converted Christian tribute-children and prisoners of war, were essential to the military success of the Ottoman state and went on to become the model for discipline in the Western armies of the sixteenth century. This infantryman is armed with the standard curved scimitar of the period and a short bow. Janissary bowmen first proved their worth at the battle of Nicopolis (1396), where they were deployed against cavalry to great effect behind stakes in a skirmishing formation. By the time of the siege of Constantinople, they were an essential part of the Ottoman Turkish army.

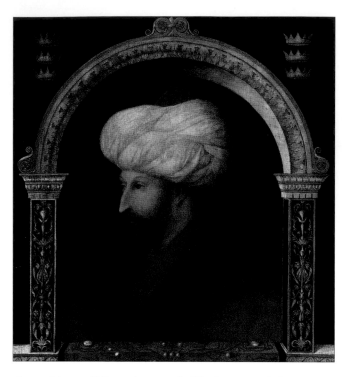

SULTAN MEHMET II FAHTI, known as the 'The Conqueror'. Italian court painter Giovanni Bellini (1430–1516) was called to Constantinople in 1479 and painted the portrait in the year before Sultan Mehmet II's death.

THE TREBUCHET was one of the major siege weapons used in the medieval period. Its long wooden arm was wound down and held in place. To the thin end was attached a sling in which the missile – usually a large rock – was placed. To the thick end was attached a very heavy weight – perhaps a crate of large stones. When released, the weight dropped, the arm was flung up, the sling was thrown over violently and the missile hurled with great force.

crumbled but the Byzantines, led by the Italian general Giustiani Longo, repaired it in time. Having ordered the moat filled Mehmed unleashed his men in the first assault, costing him 400 men. The Christians, heavily armed knights on foot led by Longo, suffered no casualties. Obviously taking Constantinople was not going to be a walkover and the defenders' morale soared.

ITALIAN REINFORCEMENTS

Two days later a small fleet of heavy and well armed Italian merchant vessels broke through the Ottoman Fleet's blockade with little trouble using artillery and Greek Fire. Their arrival with news and much needed grain boosted morale further. Mehmed, who had witnessed the defeat in person, was so enraged he fired Balthoghlu on the spot and reduced him to a common sailor.

The defenders' luck now ran out as Mehmed managed to move his galleys on rolling logs across the land side of Pera to the Golden Horn. Constantinople was now threatened from the north as well. A bravely led, but ineptly executed, night attack with fire ships failed leaving the Genoese and Venetians accusing each other of treason. Constantine XI was appalled with the Italians' behaviour telling them 'The war outside our gates is enough for us. For the pity of God do not start a war between yourselves'.

On 7 and 12 May the Turks made two failed night-time assaults against the Lycus section. Mehmed was now losing heart and his Grand Vizier, Halil Pasha, urged him to abandon the siege. Mehmed gave the old man a violent dressing down telling him that he would have the 'Apple of Rum' (i.e. Constantinople) whatever the cost and time it would take. A major threat to a city or castle under siege during this period was tunnelling. Here the Turks, thanks to Serbian expertise, had an advantage and they had begun digging a series of tunnels to undermine and blow up the Land Wall. As luck would have it the Byzantines were ably led in counter-mining by a Scottish crusader knight, Sir John Grant, whose efforts in flooding the Turkish mines neutralized these efforts.

As if this was not bad enough the defenders made a surprise night attack on 18 May and left the Turkish siege towers in flames. Five days later the defenders captured the Serbian mining master who revealed the whereabouts and depths of the remaining Turkish tunnels. This good news was tempered by the arrival of a lone Venetian galleon with the news that the Pope had not been able to collect a relief army.

BAD OMENS

During the 23 and 24 May, natural phenomena served to undermine the city's morale with devastating results. There was always the lingering fear that the city was doomed once the West would not succour the defenders. There was also the ancient prophecy that Constantinople would fall when the ruler was named Constantine and the present Emperor was named Constantine XI. During the procession to take out the Holy Icon of the Mother of God, the icon was carelessly dropped to the ground amidst gasps of disbelief and horror. Once the icon had been picked up and the procession continued its progress through the capital it was interrupted by a sudden flash flood. During the following day, 24 May, Constantinople was enveloped in a thick blanket of fog quite unheard of for this balmy month and which, the Byzantines whispered in shock to each other, hid the departure of God's protection from the city. It was God's punishment for the Orthodox allying themselves with the schematic Catholics from the West.

Morale among the besiegers was no better and again Halil Pasha forced Mehmed to agree to one final, massive assault during the night of 28/29 May. If that failed then the previously so boastful Sultan agreed he would lift the siege once and for all. By the late evening of 28 May Mehmed and his generals had completed all preparations while the defenders braced themselves for what would prove the final battle. That same evening an ecumenical Mass was held in Hagia Sophia with Constantine in attendance where Catholic and Orthodox rubbed shoulders.

THE FINAL ASSAULT

At 1.30 a.m. some 20,000 irregulars (bashi-bazouks), screaming and running at top speed, rushed the Land Wall but after two hours of bloody and merciless fighting the heavily armoured defenders had left only heaps of Turkish dead on the ground. The Anatolian army regulars failed equally miserably and assaults against the Sea Wall were also fiascos. Then, through treason or carelessness on the part of the defenders, some irregulars found that the small Kerkaporta gate between the Blachernae Palace section of the wall and the main Theodosian Wall had been left slightly ajar. Wasting no time the Turks, hundreds strong, rushed the gate and were through between the first and second walls where the few defenders were simply unable to stem the tide.

During the fighting on the main outer wall Longo was mortally wounded and instead of remaining to fight by the side of the Venetians and Byzantines he chose, with disastrous results, to be evacuated down to the port. The Genoese, who had fought until that moment with outstanding determination and bravery, saw their commander leave on a stretcher and they panicked fleeing down to the port as well. Constantine's desperate pleas for Longo to stay went unheeded and the Venetians howled that those dogs from Genoa had betrayed them!

The Turks had by this time been able to open the main gate and poured through, where small groups of defenders, including the armour-clad Constantine, were cut down where they stood. The Catalans fought with grim Hispanic fatalism secure in the knowledge that fighting the Infidel assured them a speedy passage to Heaven.

AFTERMATH

Some 4000 defenders lay dead, and it was claimed most of the population was enslaved while churches, monasteries and houses were burnt to the ground or defiled. Mehmed immediately converted Hagia Sophia into a grand mosque. The fall of Constantinople was the end of the Byzantine Empire, and established the Ottoman Turks as a threat to Europe that lasted until their failed siege of Vienna in 1683.

CROSSBOWMAN WERE MORE effective in a siege situation, and some Aragonese and Genoese crossbowmen mercenaries were employed to defend Constantinople. By this time Western plate armour had become so heavy that knights ceased using a shield, freeing them to use heavy two-handed weapons.

CONSTANTINOPLE

1 Mehmed II establishes his camp outside the Land Wall in early April 1453. The city is cut off and the walls receive a constant battering.

4 On the night of 28/29 May the Turks break in over the wall and through a small postern gate.

5 Constantine XI is killed. For three days the city is sacked and looted.

KEY

← OTTOMAN TURKS

← CHRISTIANS

3 Mehmed sends Turkish ships overland round Pera on rollers and into the Golden Horn. Constantinople is now fully blockaded.

2 A small Italian fleet breaks through and is let into the Golden Horn, giving temporary relief.

LEPANTO

In the last great Mediterranean galley battle, the combined fleet of the Western Christian powers decisively defeated the Turkish fleet thanks to superior gunnery and better-armed fighting men. The Turks' losses were so great that their naval power never really recovered.

The last Venetian stronghold, Famagusta, fell on 1 August 1571 the Turks massacring the population and brutally murdering the Venetian commander Marcantonio Bragadino – he was flayed alive and stuffed with straw. In response to the Turkish threat, Spain, the Papacy, Venice, Genoa and Malta had formed the Holy League on 25 May 1571 and mobilized their combined naval power for war. Only the acute threat from the east would have compelled Venice to make allies of her sworn enemies Genoa and Spain, while accepting a 'Spaniard' Don Juan of Austria as Grand Admiral of the Combined Fleet. Juan was the 26-year-old illegitimate half-brother of King Philip II of Spain.

As if to heighten such fears, the Sultan, Selim II, ordered his Grand Admiral (Kapudan Pasha) Ali Pasha – as young and tempestuously proud as Don Juan – to

LEPANTO FACTS

Who: Philip II of Spain and Pope Pius V founded the Holy League to fight the Ottoman Turks under Sultan Selim II. The League's Fleet was commanded by Don Juan of Austria (1545–76) while the Turks were led by Ali Pasha (d. 1571).

What: Lepanto was the greatest Christian naval victory against the Muslims and the last sea battle fought exclusively with oared galleys.

Where: In the Gulf of Patras on the western coast of Greece, taking its name from the port of Lepanto (Naupaktos).

When: 7 October 1571.

Why: The Ottoman Turkish Empire posed a deadly threat to Italy and the rest of Europe.

Outcome: Christian gunfire smashed the Ottoman fleet, breaking Turkish naval power in the Mediterranean.

THE BATTLE OF LEPANTO, *as depicted by the Venetian school of painting, the home city of some of the victors. The painting accurately portrays the crowded nature of the battle, where ships came alongside each other to exchange close fire and occasionally board to engage in hand-to-hand fighting.*

THE GREAT ARMADA 1588

The defeat of the Spanish Armada is one of the legendary victories of English history. English gunnery overcame a Spanish fleet equipped for boarding actions, but only after an attack by fireships at Calais scattered the Armada, preventing it escorting the Spanish army across the Channel.

Until 1585 King Philip II of Spain and Queen Elizabeth I had learned to live with each other. In that year, Francis Drake raided the Spanish coast while the English, now allied to the Dutch rebels, landed 4000 troops in Holland. It was a declaration of war, if not in name, then in reality against Spain. Parma suggested that he should land 30,000 men from his Army of Flanders directly on the Kent coast while Don Álvaro de Bazán, Marquis of Santa Cruz, suggested sending 510 ships and 95,000 troops against England directly from Spain. Santa Cruz had taken the

ARMADA FACTS

Who: Philip II of Spain sent the Duke of Medina Sidonia (1550–1619) with the 'invincible Armada' against Queen Elizabeth I of England whose fleet was led by Lord Howard of Effingham (1536–1624) and Sir Francis Drake (1543–96).

What: A landmark naval battle that saw the English system of sea warfare with battle lines firing broadsides introduced, eclipsing the tactics of Spanish 'galley style' warfare.

Where: The English Channel from Cornwall to Gravelines on the Belgian coast.

When: 31 July to 9 August 1588.

Why: Philip II was seeking to invade England with the Duke of Parma's

30,000-strong army and end his English problems once and for.

Outcome: A fireship attack at Calais broke up the Armada's formation, the English won the engagement at Gravelines, and the survivors of the Armada were forced to sail around the British Isles to escape.

THIS COLOURFUL HAND-TINTED ILLUSTRATION *shows the Spanish and English fleet closing with each other in the English Channel in August 1588. From a painting in the National Maritime Museum.*

LÜTZEN

1632

In one of the great battles of the Thirty Years War, the 'Lion of the North', Gustavus Adolphus of Sweden, faced a revived Imperial army under Wallenstein at Lützen. The Swedish King was killed, but his troops rallied and were victorious after a hard fight against opponents who had learnt from their previous defeats.

L ittle did the Bohemian patriots who threw the Imperial delegates out of the windows of the Hradcany Castle in Prague realize that their actions would unleash the longest and bloodiest war in modern European history, lasting a full 30 years. The Holy Roman Emperor Ferdinand II gave command of the Imperial Army to Count Albrecht von Wallenstein, a ruthless, scheming Czech nobleman, who swiftly defeated the Danes at the battle of Lutter in 1626. With an army of 125,000 men Wallenstein had won the war and secured the whole of Germany for Ferdinand II, who repaid his victories with an abrupt dismissal. Ferdinand's timing was disastrous since the triumphant Imperialists were about to meet and be crushed by their most formidable enemy, the Swedes.

LÜTZEN FACTS

Who: King Gustavus II Adolphus of Sweden (1594–1632), commanding the Swedish Army, against Prince Albrecht von Wallenstein, Prince of Friedland (1583–1634), leading the Imperial Army.

What: In a hard-fought battle, the Imperial forces showed they had learnt from their previous defeat at Swedish hands, and Gustavus was killed. However, the Swedes rallied and were victorious.

When: 6 November 1632.

Where: The fields outside the small town of Lützen near Leipzig in Saxony (eastern Germany).

Why: Wallenstein threatened Saxony – an ally of Sweden.

Outcome: The battle saved Saxony but the Thirty Years War (1618–48) ground on despite this hard won Protestant victory.

SEEN FROM NEARBY HEIGHTS, *troops manoeuvre into position as the battle of Lützen develops. The infantry columns favoured by Gustavus Adolphus can be seen forming up for the attack.*

THE SWEDISH ARMY

Gustavus II Adolphus had become King of Sweden in 1611, aged only 17, but had gained valuable experience fighting the Russians and Poles between 1611 and 1630. The young King had modernized the Swedish army and created Europe's first truly professional standing army. His artillery was modelled on that of the Dutch but used lighter, more mobile guns of standardized calibres and handled by trained professionals. Artillery was used by Gustavus Adolphus in a new offensive manner in close cooperation with the infantry, where his artillery fired eight rounds to the six fired by the musketeers.

The infantry's pikemen had their armour lightened and their pikes shortened, while the Swedish musketeers used lighter muskets. Both were grouped in mixed, flexible brigades or rectangular columns to increase mobility and speed of deployment. The baggage train was reduced to an absolute minimum to improve marching speed and campaign mobility. His cavalry, unlike the Imperial cuirassiers, were only lightly armoured and so attacked the flanks of the enemy under cover of artillery fire, charging at high speed with drawn swords.

BREITENFELD

It was thus a new but inexperienced army that was about to invade the continent of Europe for the first time in 1630. The Swedes feared that Wallenstein's army would take

HAVING PLUNGED into the mêlée to shore up a faltering brigade, the Swedish king's wounded horse carried him into the enemy ranks where, deprived of his escort, he was surrounded by Imperialist troopers and killed.

Stralsund and with the aid of privateers dominate the Baltic and perhaps even threaten Sweden itself.

On 6 July 1630 Gustavus Adolphus landed in northern Germany with 13,000 men. When the new Imperial commander, General Count Tilly (1559–1632), sacked the city of Magdeburg, Gustavus simply marched on Berlin and forced George William the Elector to join him or see his capital – like Magdeburg – burnt to the ground. When Tilly and Imperial army invaded Saxony its Elector, George John, had little choice but to become a Swedish 'ally'. Consequently, the Saxon-Swedish army of 47,000 men marched on Leipzig on 16 September, bumping into the Imperial cavalry commander Count Pappenheim (1594–1632) near a village called Breitenfeld.

Tilly, aged 73, was still a practitioner of 'Spanish' style warfare. This meant fighting your enemy in massive squares of 1500–2000 men with muskets and pikes, called *tercios* in Spanish, with heavy cavalry on either flank. He lined up his 40,000-strong army in 17 massive *tercios* with 10,000 heavy cavalry in smaller squares on the sides. Gustavus placed his Swedish and elite Finnish troops in the centre supported by three brigades of Scottish mercenaries. To the left stood General Count Horn with a mixed force of mainly German and some Swedish troops, while the entire right was made up the Elector's Saxons. The Swedish artillery fired off a massive salvo and their batteries fired three rounds to every one Imperial round.

Tilly's right wing mistook Pappenheim's unauthorized attack as a signal for a general advance against the Saxons who – seeing the invincible tercios advance – broke and fled,

GUSTAVUS ADOLPHUS understood that his horse needed firepower if they were to break their enemies and so copied the Dutch System of deploying bodies of musketeers between those of horse, a practice known as interlarding the horse. These men were thus able to defend the horsemen by outranging the pistols of the enemy horse.

their Elector in the lead. At one stroke a third of the Allied army was gone. But Gustavus' troops could move and manoeuvre twice as fast as Tilly's and the Allies quickly took the Saxons' place. The whole Imperial line began to buckle, and finally broke, leaving the field to the Swedes.

Gustavus had reignited the war and during the winter of 1631–2 he occupied much of western and southern Germany even threatening Vienna. On 16 April 1632 he caught and defeated Tilly at Lech – his enemy was dead two weeks later. In sheer desperation Ferdinand II was forced to recall Wallenstein – the only Imperial commander willing and able to put a stop to the rampaging Swedes.

THE LÜTZEN CAMPAIGN

Prospects looked good for the Imperial side, since Wallenstein was a shrewd strategist with a cool and calculating head. He avoided battle at all costs, forcing Gustavus to take the initiative and on 4 September the Allied army unsuccessfully attacked Wallenstein's fortified positions at Fürth, losing 3000 troops. Wallenstein extracted himself from his positions there and invaded Saxony but committed the mistake, on 22 October, to go into winter quarters sending his cavalry (5000 strong) under Pappenheim to Halle.

Gustavus took immediate advantage of Wallenstein's mistake and marched during 5 November as quickly as he could toward Pergau to join up with the Saxons. After 15

years of war the German countryside was ravaged and could not feed the armies and Gustavus needed a battle of annihilation to put an end to this constant movement. The Allied advance was blocked by Croat and Imperial cavalry at the Rippach stream for hours on that day which left Gustavus no choice but to move his army toward Lützen. Here the Allied (Swedish, Finnish, German and Scottish) troops spent a cold, miserable and dreary night out in the open during the night of 5/6 November with the Imperial army bivouacked only 5km (3 miles) away.

On the other side Wallenstein – so troubled with gout he had to be carried around in a sedan chair – was determined to fight a defensive battle here since he had tried his best to avoid a battle altogether. Lützen was on a flat, featureless north German plain with the main road to Leipzig running

THE DECLINE OF ARMOURED cavalry and the return of the infantryman to the centre-stage of the battlefield was accompanied by a resurrection of military drill. Here a company of pikemen is shown in three distinct formations, as it would have appeared in a military manual of the seventeenth century.

through it from south-west to the north-east atop a raised causeway that formed a natural line of defence for the Imperial side. On either side of that road was a ditch that Wallenstein's men spent 5 November and the following night making into a formidable line of trenches that would be filled with musketeers.

DISPOSITIONS

Wallenstein had 25,000 men – facing 18,000 Allies – with Pappenheim's 8000 as reinforcements and he would form his order of battle in a single line just north of the Leipzig road. His right flank rested on a knoll just north of Lützen – Windmill Hill – while his left was left hanging in the open. Yet Wallenstein had learnt the lessons of the Breitenfeld disaster well. The infantry was now more mobile and grouped in shallower, more manoeuvrable formations with their own light artillery. The three Imperial batteries, with a total of some 60 guns, were well placed and protected while the cavalry had absorbed some Swedish tactics and equipment. Wallenstein placed himself with the infantry –

WHEN ARTILLERY was first introduced in Europe it was extremely cumbersome, requiring teams of oxen, horses and men to draw each piece. Monarchs and their generals were constantly seeking better means of producing stronger, lighter cannon that could be moved with less difficulty and employed on a wider scale for both siege and battle.

in four tercios – in the middle while he placed Colloredo's cavalry on the left and Ottavio Piccolomini's cavalry on the right. He then set fire to Lützen to create a smokescreen and prevent the enemy using its houses for cover.

By the early light of a grey dawn the Swedes and their allied troops took up position opposite the Imperials. In the centre were Brahe and Kniphausen each with four infantry brigades, the right – mainly Swedes and Finns – were under Gustavus' personal command while the left was under Prince Bernhard of Saxe-Weimar (1604–39). Bernhard was a young but experienced German mercenary commander of dubious credentials as a Protestant 'patriot' and he was to show himself a good choice as deputy commander.

THE BATTLE BEGINS

The fog thickened as the morning progressed rather than thinned out as one would have expected. So the planned attack had to be postponed from 8.00 a.m. to 11.00 a.m. when the fog lifted temporarily and allowed Gustavus to begin his attack. Due to skilled and coordinated Imperial artillery and musket fire the advance was halted on the left and centre. It was only on the right where a breakthrough was achieved but at a high cost. The Swedish and Yellow Brigades managed to clear the trench of musketeers, cross the road and seize the batteries to the north of the road.

Then the fighting, as the fog descended upon the battlefield yet again, became a murderous stalemate. Just as the Imperial left crumbled, Pappenheim arrived and rescued the Imperial army from being overwhelmed by the Swedish-Finnish onslaught. The Swedish Brigade lost 70 per cent of its pikemen and 40 per cent of its musketeers in the slaughter that now ensued. The other side was just as badly mauled, as shown by Piccolomini having five horses killed under him and being wounded as many times during the fighting. The Swedish cavalry were reduced to scattered small groups on either side of the raised road and they began to waver. Only the intervention by the army's chief chaplain, Jacob Fabricius, steadied their nerves and brought them back into battle.

ALBRECHT VON WALLENSTEIN, commander of the Imperial army during the 30 Years War, is shown in this oil painting sitting on horseback. He is wearing the layered plate armour still popular with cavalrymen of the time.

THE DEATH OF GUSTAVUS ADOLPHUS

Meanwhile things had gone very wrong for the King. When Colonel Frederick Stenbock of the Småland cavalry was shot in the foot Gustavus took personal command of the unit. He rode north to aid the hard-pressed Swedish and Finnish troops north of the road. Just as they began to advance the fog descended and it was, as one Swedish soldier said, 'thick as pea soup'. Simultaneously Imperial cuirassiers smashed into the Småland regiment and everything became confused.

Since the Polish war, when a bullet had been lodged in his body, Gustavus had been unable to wear metal body armour and he wore instead thick, hardened leather. But this was hardly any protection against bullets that were flying past thick and fast. His left arm was hit, and he was forced to drop his sword and take the reins of his horse, Steiff, in his right hand, and he got separated from the Smålanders. An Imperial officer, Moritz von Falkenberg, shot Gustavus in the back, but was himself shot from his horse. One of the King's guards tried to prop up the wounded and bleeding King in his saddle but Steiff was now hit in the neck and Gustavus fell off the saddle but he was stuck with one of his feet in the stirrups. He was dragged a few yards but lay on the ground – still alive. When Piccolomini arrived to inspect the rumour that their mortal foe was dying, he gave orders to kill the King and his men did so gleefully – firing a pistol into his temple. They also stole his weapons and clothes.

Meanwhile a bloody and terrified Streiff came galloping out of the fog. The Swedish and allied troops had heard that the King was dead and feared that all was lost. Bernhard, now in command, rallied the wavering men for a counter-attack and as the Swedes advanced they found their hero King's corpse – mutilated and stripped. Bernhard had calculated that they would now thirst for revenge and so they did, more than willing to avenge Gustavus' humiliating death. The general Swedish attack had bent the Imperial line into something resembling a crescent but both sides were now tired and wearying of fighting. They came to a halt as they fired at each other but could not break the deadlock. Bernhard decided that the only way to bring this dismal battle to an end would be to attack Windmill Hill, knock out Wallenstein's remaining 13 guns and break through between the enemy's centre and left.

The Swedish batteries unleashed a storm of shot that silenced the battery atop Windmill Hill and then, at 3.00 p.m., the Swedes, Finns and other troops – with drums beating and flags waving – marched swiftly up the slope leading to the hill. They were thrown back by withering fire but regrouped and attacked again until they had seized the hill and the trenches around. These were filled with dead and dying men. Finally, after two hours of intensive fighting, the Swedish colours were raised – at 5.00 p.m. – atop the hill. The battle was won.

IMPERIAL CUIRASSIER

Cuirassiers of the Thirty Years' War continued to wear plate armour for maximum defence but had discarded the lance in favour of pistols. Their armour was usually of a good quality and could stop both sword cuts and pistol balls. It was also articulated, which means the many layers could slide over each other, allowing a lot of movement. However, it also earned them the nickname of 'lobsters'.

AFTERMATH

Wallenstein could have fought on but his troops were now utterly exhausted and demoralized. Wallenstein's son, Bertold, was one of the casualties and the whole slaughter had cost 7000 lives – some 4000 Imperial and the rest Allied.

Lützen was a Swedish-Allied victory but only just, and it was Bernhard who had led the army to victory. A year later Wallenstein was murdered while Bernhard was defeated by the Spanish and Imperial armies at Nördlingen in 1635. Amazingly the war dragged on until finally, on 24 October 1648, the exhausted combatants finally signed a lasting peace – that of Westphalia.

WITH ITS MORE EFFICIENT MECHANISM, *cavalrymen who were about to ride into combat preferred the wheel-lock pistol. Not only could such pistols be loaded easily but the user could be reasonably sure of being able to fire when they wanted to without the complicated process of using a match for ignition.*

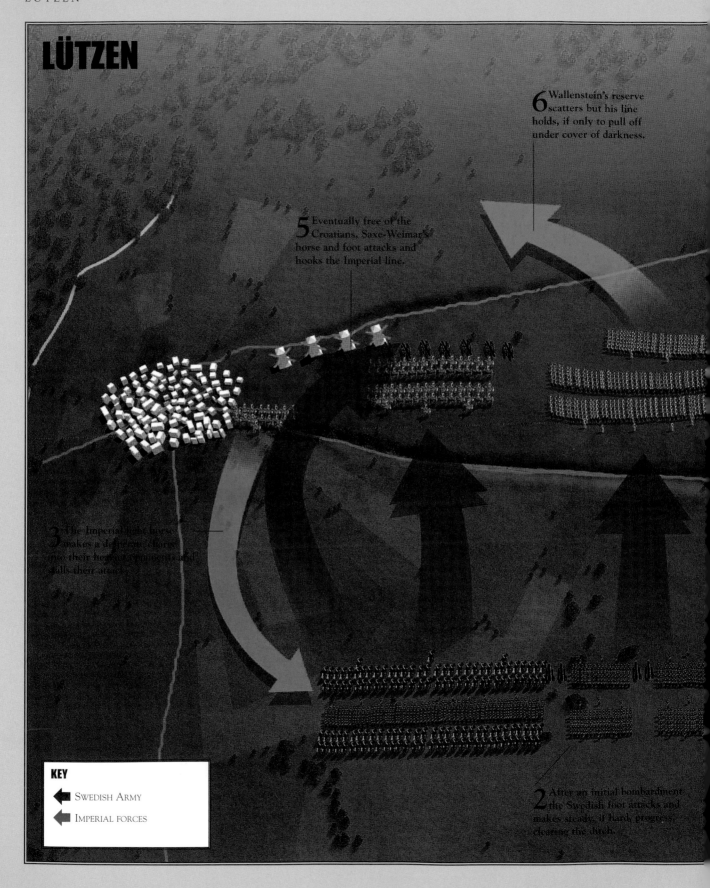

LÜTZEN

6 Wallenstein's reserve scatters but his line holds, if only to pull off under cover of darkness.

5 Eventually free of the Croatians, Saxe-Weimar's horse and foot attacks and hooks the Imperial line.

3 The Imperial light horse makes a desperate charge into their heavy opponents and stalls their attack.

KEY

SWEDISH ARMY

IMPERIAL FORCES

2 After an initial bombardment the Swedish foot attacks and makes steady, if hard, progress, clearing the ditch.

4 Pappenheim returns and repulses the Swedish horse only to become exhausted. He is replaced by Piccolomini's reserve.

1 Seeing the Imperialists advance too near the ditch to manoeuvre, the Swedish right attacks and drives them back.

BLENHEIM

1704

During the War of the Spanish Succession, the Duke of Marlborough lead a daring march across Europe to defeat a superior Franco-Bavarian force at Blenheim on the Danube. This victory secured not only the safety of the Habsburg capital, but also Marlborough's reputation as one of the great military commanders of history.

On 1 November 1700 King Carlos II of Spain died without a natural heir leaving his vast empire to the grandson of Louis XIV, Philip Duke of Anjou, to be ruled as an undivided realm, something that powers of the anti-French 'Grand Alliance' were determined to prevent. Louis XIV had no wish to provoke another war but, at the same time, he could not see an Austrian Habsburg, Archduke Charles, become King of Spain and thus leave France surrounded on all sides by enemy states. If he had wished to maintain peace yet see his grandson Philip on the Spanish throne then Louis went about it totally the wrong way. In February 1701 his armies occupied the Spanish Netherlands including some Dutch-controlled forts, thus violating a series of internationally agreed treaties and provoking his most dangerous enemy King

BLENHEIM FACTS

Who: A Franco-Bavarian army under Marshal Tallard (1652–1728) faced an Allied army under the Duke of Marlborough (1650–1722) and Prince Eugene of Savoy (1663–1736).

What: Marlborough's aggressive and shrewd battlefield tactics coupled with superior infantry firepower, stronger artillery and cavalry shock tactics marked the end of French military supremacy in the War of the Spanish Succession.

Where: At the village of Blenheim (Blindheim) on the Danube in central Bavaria.

When: 13 August 1704.

Why: The Grand Alliance sought to limit Franco-Bavarian power by decisively defeating their forces in the field.

Outcome: Marlborough and Prince Eugene of Savoy defeated the Franco-Bavarian army and thereby saved Austria from invasion.

LED BY THEIR JUNIOR OFFICERS, British infantry exchange volleys with their French counterparts before closing for hand-to-hand fighting. It was still common in the early eighteenth century for sergeants and junior officers to be armed with pikes.

William III of England and the Netherlands into a conflict neither had sought. By September 1701, in response William had revived the Grand Alliance, Austria, the Netherlands and Britain, against Louis XIV.

'CORPORAL JOHN'

Unfortunately William III was thrown from his horse and died of his injuries on 8 March 1702, leaving the throne to his sister-in-law Queen Anne (reigned 1702–14). The Anglo-Dutch alliance was now to be led by the most remarkable military and political leader of his age: Sir John Churchill, the First Duke of Marlborough. As his outstanding abilities as a field commander, politician and diplomat were to show during the war, the confidence placed in him was more than amply justified.

'Corporal John', as he was affectionally known to his troops, had realized that the development of new flintlock muskets, coupled with the replacement of the pike with the socket bayonet, had restored the offensive to infantry tactics.

THE BATTLE OF BLENHEIM TAPESTRY is displayed in the Green Writing Room at Blenheim Palace. Here, the Duke of Marlborough sits astride a white horse, in commanding posture.

Equally cavalry were to be used in massed formation, using shock tactics and charging with drawn swords. Unlike his peers therefore, Marlborough, following in the footsteps of Gustavus II Adolphus, avoided needless manoeuvring and sought a rapid decision through a fiercely-fought pitched battle to defeat the enemy with one mighty blow.

THE CAMPAIGN

By early 1704 the war, having proved indecisive for the last three years, had entered a most critical and dangerous state for the Allies. A large Franco-Bavarian army was poised to march on the Imperial capital of Vienna forcing Emperor Leopold I to recall his most brilliant and experienced commander, Prince Eugene of Savoy from Italy with his army. The Austrians also called upon their Anglo-Dutch allies to aid them.

Marlborough knew that the exposed Netherlands and the war would be lost should the enemy defeat the Imperial army and seize control of Vienna. However, the Dutch Estates General asked the English commander to move 'their' army away from the Dutch border. Marlborough placated the Dutch by claiming that he would only move

To prepare a cannon to fire, the crew would have to go through a number of stages: first, swab the barrel with a wet sponge; then, load powder into the barrel; then ram in the charge with the ramrod; next, direct the gun using a handspike; and finally, apply a lighted match to fire.

his army to the Moselle river and no further. Leaving 70,000 men to watch the Netherlands, Marlborough – with 70,000 men and 48 guns – marched south along the Rhine. He faced 60,000 French at Strasbourg and the Franco-Bavarian army of 60,000 and it was crucial, should the Allies have any hope of success, to keep these two armies apart. Hence Prince Eugene (with 30,000 men) took up position in Baden to keep Marshal Villeroi at bay while Marlborough – who had reached Donauwörth on 1 July – dealt with Marshal Marsin and the Elector of Bavaria, Prince Maximilian II Emmanuel.

Marlborough had to take this strategically-placed fortified town without a time consuming siege if he was to cross the Danube unscathed and be able to defeat the Franco-Bavarians before the campaigning season came to an end. The Bavarian Elector had sent 14,000 troops under Marshal d'Arco's command to build a fortress outside Donauwörth, called the Schellenberg, and to hold this vital river crossing against the advancing Marlborough. The Allied army, now reinforced by Prince Louis, Elector of Baden, had taken up position near the fortress by noon on 2 July. Marlborough ordered his quartermaster general to set up tents in order to create the impression that his army would attack the following day. This simple ruse worked.

At 5.00 p.m. the artillery opened fire on the Schellenberg and at 6.15 p.m. 6000 British infantry attacked in three columns, supported by cavalry, and made three unsuccessful assaults against the fortified works. D'Arco's

garrison was now pinned down giving Prince Louis the chance to attack with a second force against the northwestern side of the fortress at 7.30 p.m. The affair was now decided in vicious hand-to-hand combat between the Allied and Bavarian troops but in the end the defenders – losing a staggering 10,000 men – were overwhelmed by the force and ferocity of the assault. Marlborough suffered 1400 killed and 3800 wounded.

DISPOSITIONS

These casualties were light compared to the gains of the Allies: the road to the Danube via Nördlingen was now open. Marlborough's army crossed the Lech River on 8 July and began to lay waste to the Bavarian countryside in a brutal and systematic fashion that left no villages or farms standing in the path of the inexorably advancing Allies. Marlborough was now nearing the quarry and requested, on 11 August, that Eugene join him, especially as the experienced French Marshal Count Camille de Tallard had taken command in Bavaria.

Tallard's Franco-Bavarians had taken up position just west of the village of Blenheim (or Blindheim) on 12 August. Their camp was atop a gentle rise 1.6km (1 mile) west of the marshy brook of the Nebel that formed a soggy 'moat' facing the north and the approaching enemy. The Elector's Bavarians were stationed around Lutzingen, Marsin at Oberglau and Tallard at Blenheim. The left (west) flank rested on a series of hills and forests while the right (east) flank was anchored on the Danube.

CORNET

Strangely, in the late seventeenth century both the flag and the officer who carried it were called cornets. This one is shown 'dipping' or saluting on a special occasion that merits rosette ribbons being plaited into the horse's mane.

THE TYPICAL THREE-RANK infantry formation in use during the eighteenth century was made possible because of the use of the bayonet. Shown here are infantry prepared to receive cavalry. The front rank kneels to ward off the horsemen with the bayonet while the second and third ranks fire.

Tallard and his colleagues felt quite safe in this 'impregnable' position that resembled a fortress and they could not believe that Marlborough and Eugene would be bold or rash enough to attack them especially when they were outnumbered.

A fortress mentality is always dangerous and as Napoleon was apt to claim 'the side that stayed within their fortifications was already beaten' and this proved no exception. The enemy commanders were ruthless and bold, especially Marlborough and the fall of Donauwörth had clearly shown that not even a real fortress could stand up to 'Corporal John' and his ferocious redcoats.

At daybreak on 12 August, Marlborough made a personal reconnaissance of the enemy's position in and around Blenheim. At 2.00 a.m. on the following day the Allied army set out westward in four columns, crossed the Kessel stream at 3.00 a.m. and three hours later had reached high ground at Wolperstetten. At 7.00 a.m. the morning mist finally lifted from the field revealing to the Franco-Bavarians the unwelcome presence of the Allied army only a stone's throw from their lines. Unbelievably enough Tallard, Marsin and the Elector still believed their enemy would withdraw and it was only with some shock and horror that they realised the Allies meant business. The general alarm was sounded sending troops, horses and wagons in all directions to take up battle positions.

The Allied commanders could note with satisfaction that they had caught their blithely self-confident enemies completely by surprise and neither the Duke nor the Italian prince were the sort of commanders to squander such a chance. Some 56,000 British, Baden, Imperial and Dutch troops faced 60,000 French and Bavarians.

THIS EIGHTEENTH-CENTURY ARTILLERY piece has been limbered for movement. Artillery pieces had become lighter and more mobile when compared to cannon of the previous century.

THE BATTLE

The battle could finally begin and it did, with a massive artillery barrage from the French, at 8.30 a.m. answered with an equally ear-shattering blast in reply from the English batteries (some 90-cannon strong). Caught napping, Tallard had no time to devise a sophisticated battle plan. The Franco-Bavarians would remain on the defensive but the two armies would fight separately. Marsin would hold the centre, the Elector on the left and Tallard himself around Blenheim down to the Danube. Marsin and the Elector would hold positions right down to the banks of the Nebel while Tallard's force would hold a position some 914m (1000 yards) south of the stream. Tallard hoped that Marlborough would advance across the Nebel, get caught in the crossfire from Oberglau and Blenheim – garrisoned with French troops – and thereby allow Tallard to counter-attack and drive the British into the marshlands flanking the Nebel.

Marlborough had noticed that the enemy's right was stronger than its left and it was therefore on the stronger flank he would attack. Marlborough had a hunch about Tallard's ruse and sent Eugene to pin down the Elector while he advanced to neutralize the French garrisons at Blenheim and Oberglau. The British and French artillery duelled for four hours while Lord Cutts' column, rushing across five pontoon bridges, crossed the Nebel and created a bridgehead on the southern bank. Marlborough awaited impatiently for news that Eugene – who was finding the country toward Lutzingen rough going – had attacked and pinned down the Elector's Bavarians before he attacked.

At long last the Savoyard's ADC arrived with the welcome news and at 12.30 p.m. Marlborough told his generals 'Gentlemen, to your posts'. Fifteen minutes later General Rowe's British brigade attacked Blenheim where – quite uselessly – 12,000 French troops were bottled up. Two assaults, in which Rowe and a third of his men were killed, were beaten back but had served their purpose. In the centre Prince Holstein-Beck's Germans attacking Oberglau were in trouble until Marlborough got Austrian cavalry from Eugene to beat back the French cavalry with heavy losses. Holstein-Beck drove the French back to the village and kept them confined there for the rest of the battle.

By 3.00 p.m. the Elector was kept away from joining the French while the villages had been prevented from supporting Tallard's counter-attack. Marlborough finally crossed with the rest of his army an hour later and at 4.30 p.m. came the welcome news that Eugene had driven the Elector from Lutzingen. Tallard finally realised that Marlborough had outmanoeuvred him and rushed nine battalions to hold the position near Oberglau. It was 'too little, too late'. The battalions fought ferociously to hold their positions but were slaughtered to the last man where they stood while the much vaunted French cavalry fled into the waters and marshy banks of the Danube. By 5.30 p.m. the battle was over, with Tallard having fallen into British hands and the whole Franco-Bavarian army having ceased to exist as an organized military force. To their lasting honour the French garrisons of Blenheim and Oberglau held out until 9.00 p.m. when they too had finally had enough of the slaughter.

AFTERMATH

It had been neither an easy victory nor a bloodless one. A fifth of the Allied army was gone – 4500 killed and 7500 wounded – but this was nothing to the destruction wrought on the Franco-Bavarians who had lost 15,000 prisoners and 13,600 dead, wounded, and drowned in the Danube.

Marlborough had marched his army without the French being able to intercept or block his advance 400km (250 miles) into the heart of the enemy's territory, and gained one of the greatest victories in European military history, a victory that could be compared to Agincourt as France's reputation for military excellence and invincibility had been destroyed again. Europe was saved from French hegemony.

BRITISH OFFICERS

In order to defray the cost of maintaining large armies, monarchs often sold commissions. The more prestigious the rank and position, the greater was the purchase price. Although uniforms were standard by the eighteenth century, embellishments were initially permitted to reflect the individual's social and military stature. On the left is a British general, in the centre an officer of engineers and on the right a British Field Marshal. The latter appeared to prefer a less ostentatious display of his rank.

BLENHEIM

3 Prince Eugene sends his army against the whole of Max Emmanuel's position, preventing him from giving assistance to Tallard.

6 The collapse of Tallard's position compels Max Emmanuel to abandon his rally and withdraw his forces.

5 Tallard's cavalry charges Marlborough's forces as they cross the Nebel stream, but are repulsed with heavy losses, as the weight of the British attack falls upon the outnumbered French cavalry.

2 Holstein-Beck's German battalions attack Oberglau. The Germans manage to wrest the town on the second try.

4 Marlborough's main attack falls on Tallard's centre. The French marshal deployed two ranks of cavalry with few infantry in reserve.

1 Marlborough attacks Blenheim with 20 battalions, pinning much of Tallard's infantry, deployed in and around the town.

KEY

⬅ ALLIED ARMY

⬅ FRANCO-BAVARIAN ARMY

SARATOGA

In the autumn of 1777, the British Major General John Burgoyne moved his army southward through the rebellious colony of New York, toward Albany, in the main thrust of a three-pronged offensive. Rather than victory, Burgoyne found frustration, hardship and eventually surrender following a series of battles which ended at Saratoga.

With the colonial rebellion in its third year, the Continental Army under General George Washington (1732–99) had accomplished precious little against the stalwart British. The redcoats occupied the city of New York and had seized the initiative. Only the minor victories at Trenton and Princeton the previous December lifted the rebel spirits, countering the memories of repeated reverses on the battlefield and a harsh winter encampment at Morristown, New Jersey. What the British could not destroy from without, rivalry and jealousy among the American commanders threatened to destroy from within. The Revolutionary leader John Adams (1735–1826) called 1777 the 'year of the hangman' because its

SARATOGA FACTS

Who: The British General John Burgoyne (1722–92) and a force of British regulars, Indians and German mercenaries numbering 8000 faced 7000 Continental soldiers and frontier riflemen under the command of General Horatio Gates (1727–93) and subordinates Benedict Arnold (1741–1801) and Daniel Morgan (1736–1802).

What: In the climax of his ill-fated campaign, Burgoyne was compelled to surrender the remnants of his army at Saratoga following crushing defeats at the battles of Freeman's Farm and Bemis Heights.

Where: Eastern New York in the valley of the Hudson River north of Albany.

When: 17 October 1777.

Why: The British determined a grand strategy to split New England, the hotbed of revolutionary ardour, from the remaining colonies.

Outcome: The turning point of the American war for independence, the surrender of an entire British army in the field at Saratoga convinced France to enter the conflict on the side of the Americans.

MARKSMAN IN ACTION: *while soldiers of other military units look on, a buckskin-clad member of Morgan's Riflemen demonstrates his marksmanship skills during a training exercise.*

SARATOGA

6 Against the wishes of his officers, Burgoyne chooses the following day to negotiate terms of surrender with the Americans, ending the disastrous campaign.

5 His situation desperate, General John Burgoyne orders the remaining British forces to withdraw northward along the river road toward the village of Saratoga.

4 Initially repulsed, the Americans eventually capture a pair of British redoubts. While directing the effort, Arnold is seriously wounded in the leg by a musket ball.

3 Without orders, General Benedict Arnold reaches the field and directs the Colonials in pursuit of the routed British and their accompanying Hessian mercenaries.

2 Daniel Morgan's frontier riflemen spearhead a devastating assault on the British left, while 800 more Colonials assail their exposed right flank.

1 From a high bluff above the Hudson River at Bemis's Tavern, General Horatio Gates observes 1500 British troops in three columns advancing toward his left flank.

KEY

← AMERICAN FORCES

← BRITISH FORCES

TRAFALGAR 1805

Nelson's victory at Trafalgar finally ended the threat of French invasion of the British Isles and secured the Royal Navy's dominance of the seas for the next 100 years. But at the moment of his greatest triumph, Britain's foremost naval hero was killed on the deck of his flagship HMS Victory.

Nelson's victory at Trafalgar 200 years ago is the most famous and decisive naval battle of all times. But, often forgotten, is that it was the product of Napoleon's plans to invade Britain. By the spring of 1805 Napoleon had assembled some 2000 gunboats and transports in the French Channel ports to ferry an army of 167,000 veteran troops to the coast of Kent. For the invasion to succeed Napoleon had to be sure the Royal Navy was safely lured out of the Channel when his ramshackle flotilla of barges and flat-bottomed boats sailed out of Boulogne and Calais.

Napoleon had a justified contempt for his own navy but this time he needed its support if he was to destroy his most dangerous foe. Unfortunately, Napoleon had a knack for appointing the wrong men to crucial posts when it came to sea warfare and

TRAFALGAR FACTS

Who: The combined Franco-Spanish fleet of 33 ships of the line under Admiral Pierre Villeneuve (1763–1806) versus a British fleet of 27 ships of the line under Vice Admiral Lord Horatio Nelson (1758–1805).

What: Nelson's head-on attack on the Franco-Spanish line broke their formation and allowed the superior gunnery of the British ships to destroy the enemy in detail.

Where: At the western entrance to the Straits of Gibraltar off Cape Trafalgar, Spain.

When: 21 October 1805.

Why: Nelson, having chased the Franco-Spanish Fleet around the world, caught up with it in the Straits of Gibraltar and

Villeneuve chose – for personal reasons – to fight rather than flee.

Outcome: The Combined Fleet, despite heroic resistance, was smashed and Britain had removed, for good, the threat of a French invasion.

THIS PRINT, after the painting, 'Trafalgar' by William Overend, was published in the Illustrated Sporting and Dramatic News in 1905 with the title, '"The Hero of Trafalgar" Nelson on Board the Victory, October 21st 1805'. Nelson is shown standing on the right on the deck of the Victory, facing fixedly ahead while the battle rages around him.

AUSTERLITZ 1805

A year after his coronation as Emperor, in the culmination of the greatest campaign of his career, Napoleon defeated the combined armies of Russia and Austria at Austerlitz, where he, his generals and superbly trained troops displayed their prowess on the battlefield. But for all its genius, the victory at Austerlitz did not immediately bring peace.

Napoleon's campaign against the Third Coalition powers in late 1805 must be regarded as his greatest and that the battle itself Austerlitz in Bohemia a masterpiece of Napoleonic military leadership. The Allies (Austria, Britain, Russia, Sweden and Naples) were certain of the swift and overwhelming defeat of Napoleon's brash, post-revolutionary army and parvenu 'Empire'. William Pitt and Tsar Alexander I, the two main architects of this the largest coalition ever created against France, were going to attack Napoleon with 400,000 troops on a broad front stretching from Naples in the Mediterranean to Hanover and Pomerania on the Baltic. Napoleon could only hope to prevail if he moved fast, struck hard and divided

AUSTERLITZ FACTS

Who: The Emperor Napoleon (1769–1821) with 73,000 men defeat the combined armies of Imperial Russia, led by Tsar Alexander I (1777–1825), and Austria lead by Emperor Francis II (1768–1835) totalling 85,000 troops.

What: Napoleon provoked the Allies into launching an attack on ground of his choosing, then occupied the Prätzen Heights in the centre of the battlefield, dividing the enemy and defeating them.

Where: Near the village of Austerlitz in Bohemia, 113km (70 miles) north of Vienna.

When: 2 December 1805.

Why: The new revolutionary state in France and Napoleon's usurpation of the French throne were deeply threatening to the established monarchies of Europe who suspected that Napoleon sought to establish French hegemony across the continent.

Outcome: The Allied army was shattered. The French held the field, having dealt a major blow to the Third Coalition.

IN THIS OIL PAINTING NAPOLEON is seen inspecting and encouraging his troops in their bivouacs during the night prior to the battle on 2 December 1805 (by Baron Louis Albert Bacler D'Albe [1761-1848]).

AUSTERLITZ

BRUNN

2 To Napoleon's keen intelligence this strategy seemed obvious. He left Legrand and Davout with barely 20,000 men holding the right while he would concentrate the rest of his army (60,000) on the left.

3 Crucially, the Allied advance was held up and this delay fatally compromied their overly complex plan of attack, enabling a fraction of the French army to hold up their main advance while Napoleon made his plans to attack the empty Prätzen Heights.

RIVER SCHWARZAWA

PRÄTZEN HEIGHTS

5 The battle was lost even though the Allies went on fighting for hours, especially around Sokolnitz village. When they retreated the French were too tired and cold to pursue. Yet they and their Emperor had won France's greatest victory on the battlefield.

SOKOLNITZ

4 Soult's Corps marched up the heights and before the Allies realised what had happened seized this crucial position at the centre of the battlefield. Too late, Kutuzov, sent General Miloradovich to retake the heights but repeated assaults failed to dislodge the stubborn French defenders.

AUSTERLITZ

1 The Allied grand strategy was simple and effective – at least on paper. While Bagration in the north diverted Napoleon's attentions, the bulk of the Russo-Austrian army would attack from the Pratzen Heights and link up behind Napoleon's lines with Kollowrath's Corps.

KEY
◀ FRENCH ARMY
◀ RUSSIAN & AUSTRIAN FORCES

WATERLOO 1815

The final battle of the Napoleonic Wars saw the French Emperor's ambitions crushed once and for all. Despite flashes of his former brilliance in the campaign, Napoleon was unable to break up the Allied armies, and his fate was sealed by the Prussians marching to Wellington's aid on 18 June rather than falling back after their reverse at Ligny.

Revolutionary, then Napoleonic, France had been fighting Britain and her allies for 20 years when, finally, Napoleon abdicated in April 1814 and was exiled to the island of Elba. But discontent in France with the Bourbon King, Louis XVIII, led to Napoleon risking a passage from the island with 1000 men for France, where he landed on 1 March 1815. Louis was forced to flee to Belgium while the Allies began to mobilize their armies. Napoleon sincerely wished for peace but the other European powers could never permit him to threaten peace again and he was therefore obliged to mobilize eight corps. Tired of war and bloodshed the French were reluctant to pay taxes and place recruits at the Emperor's disposal. The troops were

WATERLOO FACTS

Who: The Emperor Napoleon (1769–1821) with 72,000 men of the French Armée du Nord attacked an Anglo-Netherlandish army of 60,000 men under the Duke of Wellington (1769–1852), who was joined by Prince Gebhard von Blücher's Prussian army that evening.

What: In a superb defensive battle, Wellington's army was able, with great difficulty, to hold off Napoleon's disjointed attacks until the Prussian army arrived.

Where: The ridge of Mont St Jean, near the village of Waterloo, 16km (10 miles) south of Brussels in Belgium.

When: 18 June 1815.

Why: Napoleon's escape from Elba and restoration of the Empire could not be tolerated by the Allies, who sought to crush this threat to European peace.

Outcome: Defeat at Waterloo forced Napoleon's second abdication, after which he was finally exiled to St Helena in the South Atlantic.

A CLASSICAL PAINTING *of Marshal Ney's cuirassiers with foaming horses and waving black plumes riding with death-defying courage against the indomitable squares of red-coated infantry.*

weary as were the officers and even Napoleon's own marshals – most of whom owed their rank and wealth to his patronage – were reluctant to fight. This was especially true of Ney who disliked Napoleon as a tyrant who would plunge France into new and dangerous adventures. Ney, who had first promised Louis to bring back Napoleon in an iron cage before going over to him, felt deep down that Napoleon was a spent force and that France, facing a hostile European coalition, could not prevail. Unfortunately for Napoleon his irreplaceable Chief of Staff from the old days, Marshal Berthier, had died in a accident and his replacement Marshal Soult was not so talented. The combination of Napoleon's physical and mental decline, coupled with the bungling of his subordinates Soult and Ney would lead to defeat at Waterloo.

THE ALLIED ARMIES

On the opposite side Wellington was not having a smooth run either. His Peninsular veterans were dispersed across the world or had been demobilized. As a consequence Wellington was reduced to fighting Napoleon with a motley army of Dutch, Belgian, German mercenaries (Hessians and Nassauers) and a small force of British troops – many of whom were raw recruits. He had 68,800 infantry and 14,500 cavalry making a grand total of 92,300 troops divided into three infantry corps

95TH RIFLES

In the British Army and the British expeditionary army in Belgium of 1815, the 95th Rifles stood out for two glaringly simple reasons. Firstly, its infantrymen were equipped with rifles, rather than the rest of the Army's trusted Brown Bess muskets. Secondly, when the rest of the army, irrespective of arm, wore the King's vivid scarlet uniforms the 95th clothed, for reason of camouflage, in dark-hued green. They were formed during the Peninsula War (1808–14) for a dual purpose – to fight as regular infantry and also as skirmishers and snipers ahead of the main army.

commanded by himself, General Hill and the Dutch Prince of Orange. The cavalry was under the command of the Earl of Uxbridge who doubled as Wellington's second-in-command. Relations between the two men were frosty – Uxbridge had eloped with Wellington's sister-in-law – and had been appointed against Wellington's express wishes.

The Allies were therefore relying on the Prussians with 130,000 men to stem Napoleon. Their legendary commander, Field Marshal Prince Gebhard von Blücher (1742–1819) may never have been the greatest of strategists given his troops' nickname for him – Alte Forwärts ('Old Forwards'), but he could be relied upon to fight the French and come to the aid of Wellington who expected Napoleon to attempt to drive a wedge between their separate armies.

QUATRE BRAS AND LIGNY

On 15 June Napoleon crossed the frontier into Belgium with 123,000 men in his Armée du Nord at Charleroi – exactly where Wellington had not expected him to strike. 'Napoleon has humbugged me, by God' was Wellington's comment as he rushed to assist his troops holding Marshal Ney at the crossroads of Quatre Bras. Ney had showed uncharacteristic lethargy by failing to occupy this vital position, compounding this error by only opening the battle in the afternoon and then using 4000 cuirassiers to charge the British infantry squares. Obviously Ney had, three days later at Waterloo, a complete loss of memory as he repeated that mistake – charging unbroken infantry formations without infantry support.

That same day, 16 June, the main battle took place at Ligny between Napoleon's main army of 71,000 men and Blücher's 84,000 Prussians. The Prussians had chosen to overextend themselves across marshy ground but Napoleon was not at his tactical best either. He delayed the battle until the afternoon when he was obliged to simply sledgehammer the Prussian lines into submission. For almost two hours savage fighting went on, often hand-to-hand with bayonets and firing at point-blank range. Prussian losses amounted to 19,000 and while Blücher quit the field Napoleon had sustained heavy losses – some 14,000 men – that he could ill afford. Napoleon sent Marshal Grouchy in pursuit of the Prussians with 30,000 men, but Grouchy failed to press the enemy closely, and far from retreating back to Germany as Napoleon had expected, Blücher marched west to support Wellington as he had promised.

Having beaten the Prussians Napoleon rushed to Quatre Bras where he found the British, having held off Ney's attacks, withdrawing from the battlefield in an orderly fashion, without any effort on the part of the French to pursue or harass them. Ney and his staff were sitting down for supper instead. Napoleon could not believe his eyes and gave his officers a violent dressing down that while it was deserved did nothing to raise Ney's morale. Fatally, Ney would remember this latest humiliation at Waterloo and acting upon his own initiative show that he was as dynamic as ever.

MONT ST JEAN

There was a much-needed lull the following day as Wellington's army numbering 74,300 troops in total took up position around the farm of Mont St Jean and the village of Waterloo where Wellington set up his headquarters. Wellington faced a French army of 74,500 men that had set up camp south of the road to Brussels while Napoleon, in spite of his superstitious frame of mind, had set up his headquarters at the inn of 'La Belle Alliance'.

The two armies may have been almost exactly and evenly matched numerically. This, however, took no account for the vitally qualitative differences between the two armies. Napoleon's troops were seasoned veterans where most of Wellington's men were recently recruited troops and only 28,000 of these were British – they too in great part newly-recruited men. Furthermore the French had not only more cavalry and artillery but what they had was of far greater quality than Wellington's. Not only did the French 12-pounder have a superior range to the British 9-pounder but the crews handling them were more experienced and better led. Perhaps this was a due to the simple fact that Napoleon, now an emperor, had once been a young artillery officer whose handling of the French guns at Toulon in 1793 had, quite literally, shot him to fame? Wellington was, by contrast, an infantry commander.

DISPOSITIONS

As battlefields go, that of Waterloo, compared to Borodino (1812) in Russia, was a very compact and dense one where there was to be a lot of action in a compressed space in the course of a single day. A day, 18 June, that was to change the course of European history forever.

Wellington had drawn up his army based on divisions divided into three corps. His extreme left flank was secured by the German division of the Prince of Saxe-Weimar backed by Uxbridge's cavalry to their rear. On the opposite side – on the extreme right – the Prince of Orange's Dutch-Belgian division, then came

ON THE LEFT A BROODING, slouched Napoleon contrasts in a second oil painting with the determined look and fit frame of Wellington. The reality was that they were two of best generals of their era, both determined to win.

Clinton's division (behind the Braine l'Allend road), Cooke's division, at the junction of the Brussels road Alten's division (facing the farm of La Haie) with Wellington's Reserve Corps and finally, strung out along the Ohain road, General Picton's division – the finest, with Clinton's , in the

IN THEIR CHARACTERISTIC bearskin caps, florid whiskers and sideburns, the veterans of the Old Guard was Napoleon's last reserve – one that he threw away at Waterloo.

WATERLOO

3 At 2.00 p.m. Napoleon sends d'Erlon's 1st Corps against Wellington's left-centre position. Despite massive artillery support and dashing élan the combination of General Picton's Anglo-Hanoverian infantry and the British cavalry halted the onslaught.

5 The first Prussians begin to arrive at the battlefield. Led by General von Bülow and von Zeithen, they distract Napoleon from the main battle and force him to detach more troops to stop their advance.

6 As evening closes in, with Prussian pressure increasing, Napoleon sends his precious veterans of the Imperial Guards against Wellington. Their attack is repelled and ends in a massacre – the battle is lost for the French and the Allies are united by 8.30 p.m.

2 After an artillery barrage, Prince Jérôme Bonaparte attacked the pivotal farmhouse of Hougoumont with four regiments of infantry as news arrived that the Prussians had been spotted nearby. Napoleon detached troops under Count Lobau to block their advance.

HOUGOUMONT

LA HAIE S

MONT-ST-JEAN

1 Napoleon hoped to defeat Wellington before Blücher's Prussians could come to the rescue by attacking the Allied army's frontline at La Haie Sainte, occupying the crossroads behind that position, and then driving the Allied army back to Mont Saint-Jean village.

4 ...charges with his cavalry on the slope against Wellington's massed infantry, in particular squares held together by a rigid discipline and propped by Hanoverian and Belgian reinforcements. Ney launches wave after wave of attacks and almost breaks the squares.

KEY

Anglo-Dutch forces

French Imperial forces

Prussian forces

ANTIETAM 1862

In the countryside of western Maryland, the bloodiest single day of warfare in American history ended with a tactical draw but a strategic victory for the Union as the Confederate invasion of the North was thwarted. Issued after the battle, the Emancipation Proclamation transformed the American Civil War into a crusade for human rights.

The summer of 1862 was one of frustration in Washington, DC. Sixteen months after the first shot of the American Civil War had been fired at Fort Sumter, the Union was still without a major victory in the Eastern theatre. The Peninsula Campaign, its objective the Confederate capital at Richmond, Virginia, had been repulsed during the Seven Days' Battles in June and July. A humiliating defeat at Second Manassas (Bull Run) followed at the end of August. Desperate to restore order and morale among the dispirited troops, President Abraham Lincoln reinstated General George B. McClellan to overall command. A superb organizer, McClellan was the architect of the Army of the Potomac, but he was also cautious

ANTIETAM FACTS

Who: The 55,000-man Confederate Army of Northern Virginia, commanded by General Robert E. Lee (1807–70), confronted General George B. McClellan (1826–85) and the Union Army of the Potomac, which numbered more than 85,000.

What: From dawn to dusk, Union and Confederate troops fought to a tactical draw in a three-phase battle ranging north to south from a cornfield to a sunken road and a stone bridge.

Where: Western Maryland near the town of Sharpsburg and along the banks of Antietam Creek.

When: 17 September 1862.

Why: The Confederate Army of Northern Virginia invaded Maryland, carrying the American Civil War into Northern territory.

Outcome: Lee was forced to abandon the offensive, President Abraham Lincoln changed the character of the war with the issuance of the Emancipation Proclamation, and the chance of European intervention on behalf of the Confederacy was eliminated.

IN THIS ROMANTICIZED *artist's conception of the Battle of Antietam, Union and Confederate troops are locked in combat at close quarters along the banks of Antietam Creek in western Maryland. In the background, their banner unfurled, Union soldiers and their mounted officers charge across the Lower Bridge spanning the stream and into a hail of Confederate rifle fire.*

and devoid of initiative on the battlefield. On the other hand, the Confederate Army of Northern Virginia, always hungry, often without shoes, nevertheless displayed the spirit and dash that only victory could bring. Its commander, General Robert E. Lee, had displayed tactical brilliance and defeated the enemy at nearly every turn. Only a week after Second Manassas, he crossed the Potomac River and invaded the North.

LEE'S AUDACIOUS GAMBLE

Lee reckoned that an expedition into Maryland and Pennsylvania could accomplish a great deal, both militarily and politically, for the beleaguered South. It was believed that Southern sympathizers in Maryland would rally to the rebel army, providing food, supplies and new recruits. The Confederates could also live off the rich farmland of southern Pennsylvania, destroy the railroad bridge across the Susquehanna River and threaten the state capital at Harrisburg. A victory on Northern soil would allow Lee to menace Philadelphia, Baltimore and Washington, DC. Perhaps most important of all, such a victory might bring formal recognition and much-needed assistance from the governments of Great Britain and France. Lee further realized that the capacity of the Union to wage war was virtually limitless. The Confederacy had seized the initiative. Now, it had to utilize that initiative to its fullest.

Following the abortive Peninsula Campaign, McClellan had been demoted in favour of General John Pope (1822–92), who had established and quite probably embellished his reputation as an Indian fighter in the West. During the campaign of Second Manassas, Pope may have been willing to fight, but Lee and his capable subordinates James Longstreet (1821–1904) and Thomas J. 'Stonewall' Jackson (1824–63) made him appear a rank amateur. Confederate cavalry raided Pope's headquarters at Manassas, stealing his dress coat and $350,000 in cash. Then Longstreet and Jackson completed the rout on the old battlefield of Bull Run. When Lincoln swallowed his pride and recalled McClellan, the soldiers of the Army of the Potomac gave a mighty cheer. To a man, they loved 'Little Mac'. This time, though, McClellan did not march his troops into Virginia. He headed northwest into Maryland to intercept the invading rebels.

THE CAMPAIGN

As the Confederates advanced toward the town of Frederick, Maryland, the Federal arsenal at Harpers Ferry lay between Lee and his supply base at Winchester, Virginia. It might also sever his line of communication with Richmond via the Shenandoah Valley.

Discounting one of the principles of command, Lee divided his army in the face of an enemy of superior strength

THE USE OF ARTILLERY played a significant role in the Battle of Antietam, particularly the rifled cannon used by Union units. Rifled artillery proved much more accurate than the smooth-bore cannon of the Confederates.

and sent Jackson to capture Harpers Ferry. Lee counted on McClellan's caution, confident that Jackson could complete his task and rejoin the main army before Union troops arrived in overwhelming numbers. By 12 September, the entire Army of Northern Virginia could concentrate at Hagerstown, Maryland, and continue into Pennsylvania.

While Jackson dealt with Harpers Ferry, Longstreet's corps headed for Hagerstown on 10 September. Three days later, as the bulk of McClellan's army reached Frederick, a private from an Indiana regiment noticed an envelope lying on the ground. Inside were three cigars and a copy of Special Order 191, which Lee had issued on 9 September. The order detailed the dispositions of Confederate troops, and it was soon in McClellan's possession.

Lee's entire army was now in great peril. If McClellan moved swiftly eastward through the passes in South Mountain, he might interpose his army between Longstreet at Hagerstown and Jackson at Harpers Ferry. His larger force could then crush these separate elements one at a time.

Unaware that Special Order 191 had fallen into McClellan's hands, Lee had already begun to worry that the capture of Harpers Ferry was taking too long. He knew that McClellan was at Frederick, and the movement of the Union force, although ponderously slow, still proceeded at a disturbing pace. Even with the knowledge of Lee's predicament, McClellan wasted several precious hours and did not start toward the South Mountain passes in earnest until the morning of the 14th.

Events now seemed to be developing rapidly, and Lee could feel his control of the situation slipping away. He ordered Longstreet to send troops from Hagerstown to defend Turner's and Fox's Gaps and Jackson to dispatch a force from Harpers Ferry to guard Crampton's Gap further south. Their delaying actions could buy precious time for Lee to gather his scattered forces. Inevitably, though, McClellan would force his way through the gaps, and Lee issued orders on the night of the 14th to abandon the Harpers Ferry positions in preparation for a general withdrawal to the safety of Virginia.

In the early hours of the next day, as Union troops marched ever closer, Lee finally received some good news. A message from Jackson stated that Harpers Ferry would fall on the morning of the 15th. Lee cancelled his original order and instructed his forces to concentrate near the town of Sharpsburg. Longstreet moved, and Jackson rapidly departed Harpers Ferry, leaving General A.P. Hill's Light Division to deal with captured booty and nearly 12,000 Union prisoners.

DISPOSITIONS

Believing he might yet salvage his campaign, Lee chose to make a stand along a low ridge which overlooked Antietam Creek. General J.E.B. Stuart's cavalry screened the left flank of the Confederate line, which was anchored by General John Bell Hood's division on a forested area called the West Woods and around a whitewashed Dunker Church, which stood adjacent to the Hagerstown Turnpike. General D.H. Hill placed five brigades in the rebel centre, across the Boonsborough Pike. The division of General D.R. Jones held a mile of the Confederate line, which ended along high bluffs on the west side of Antietam Creek above the lower bridge, one of three stone spans which crossed the stream. By the evening of the 16th, most of Jackson's troops had arrived from Harpers Ferry and doubled the size of Lee's force to about 36,000.

At midday on the 15th, McClellan had assembled 75,000 troops east of the Antietam. Both sides had placed artillery on the surrounding high ground, and sporadic firing

CONFEDERATE DEAD, probably from the Louisiana brigade of General Harry T. Hays, lie sprawled beside a rail fence along the Hagerstown Turnpike at Antietam. These soldiers had been locked in combat with elements of the Union Iron Brigade, commanded by General John Gibbon.

UNION INFANTRY

Ranks of well-equipped Union infantrymen march towards the sound of the guns. Although the Union Army of the Potomac consisted of some units from the standing United States Army, a large number of the soldiers were volunteers and draftees. Many of these were farmers and woodsmen from the primarily agricultural areas of the North and Midwest or European immigrants, predominantly Irish and German, from the crowded urban areas of major Northern cities.

occurred on the 16th, while McClellan refined his plan of attack. Two army corps, under Generals Joseph Hooker and Joseph K.F. Mansfield were placed on the Union right and ordered to make the initial assault, with the corps of Generals William B. Franklin and Edwin V. Sumner available to exploit any significant gains. General Fitz-John Porter's corps took up positions in the Union centre along the Boonsborough Pike, and the corps of General Ambrose Burnside was positioned on the left near the lower bridge. McClellan's plan was simple. If Hooker and Mansfield made significant gains, Burnside would attack the Confederate right flank and perhaps push on into the town of Sharpsburg. Finally, Porter's troops would assault the Confederate centre in support of either flank attack. In typical fashion, McClellan had squandered opportunities to attack the much smaller Confederate army on the afternoon of the 15th and again in the 16th. When battle was finally joined on the 17th, Lee was able to utilize his interior lines. Shuffling reinforcements to areas of heavy fighting, he stymied several Union breakthroughs. McClellan failed to coordinate his attacks and committed reserves in a piecemeal manner, negating his numerical superiority.

THE BATTLE

At first light, Hooker's Federals advanced down the Hagerstown Turnpike toward the Dunker Church. Artillery fire tore great gaps in the ranks of the defending

ABOVE: THE PERCUSSION *rifle musket, extremely accurate with its grooved barrel and large calibre bullet, inflicted heavy losses on both sides during the Civil War.*

THE MODEL 1860 Army Colt revolver was a *favourite sidearm among officers and cavalrymen in both the Union and Confederate armies.*

UNION SOLDIERS *move about their encampment. Often, army camps included 'followers' such as merchants, family members, and, in the case of the Union Army, freed slaves. The close quarters of army encampments were also environments which fostered the spread of communicable diseases. During the Civil War, many more soldiers died of disease than as a result of combat.*

Confederates, and the focus of the savage fighting became a 30-acre field of head-high corn owned by a farmer named David Miller. Relieved during the night by two brigades under General Alexander Lawton, Hood's Texans were cooking breakfast when the fighting began. A desperate Lawton called for help, and Hood's shock troops sent Hooker's spearhead reeling back more than 365m (400 yards). Both sides committed additional reinforcements, and the dead and wounded began to pile up. Some accounts relate that the bloody cornfield changed hands up to 15 times.

More than 90 minutes after Hooker's opening attacks, Mansfield assaulted the Confederates over the same ground. As his right was torn apart by Confederate artillery, Mansfield was mortally wounded. One Union division, commanded by General George Greene, managed to reach the rocky ground before the Dunker Church, but no other units appeared to take advantage of the gain, and Greene's men were isolated and pinned down.

At approximately 9.00 a.m., Sumner himself led two divisions from the vicinity of the East Woods, about half a mile from the ragged Confederate line. In response, Jackson deployed reserves, some just off the march from Harpers Ferry and others transferred from the rebel right near the stone bridge, to spring a trap along the edge of the West Woods. During the march, the second Union division, under William French, lost contact with Sumner and veered away. A single division of 5000 men, commanded by General John Sedgwick, continued, stumbling into the trap set by Jackson. The crossfire of nearly 10,000 Confederate muskets cut down half of Sedgwick's strength in a mere 20 minutes. Jackson counter-attacked but was repulsed by Sedgwick's artillery. The third Union attack of the morning had gained nothing, and scores of dead and wounded littered the ground around the cornfield, the Hagerstown Pike and the Dunker Church. By 10.00 a.m., the Confederate left had held, battered but unbroken.

The fighting now shifted southward, where D.H. Hill had taken advantage of a sunken road, which had been worn down by years of wagon traffic and now offered a natural defensive position. When French's division had marched away from Sedgwick, it had become engaged with troops from three brigades of Hill's division, which had pulled back from the fighting around the Dunker Church. A spirited battle erupted on the left of the sunken road. The famed Irish Brigade assaulted the Confederates, many of whom were from North Carolina and Alabama, in the sunken road around 10:30 a.m., suffering 540 dead and wounded before falling back. Still, the Union attacks continued. Exhausted, the Confederates began to falter when a pair of New York regiments managed to flank the sunken road and pour deadly fire down the length of the trench and a misunderstood order resulted in an entire rebel brigade abandoning its positions.

Confederate bodies were heaped two and three deep in the sunken road, which came to be known to history as 'Bloody Lane'. Once again, the Union army stood on the brink of a decisive victory. A patchwork defence slowed the Union tide, which had reached up to 548m (600 yards) beyond the sunken road. One more push with fresh troops from his ample reserve might win the day for McClellan, but the commander hesitated and then ordered his troops to hold their positions.

From morning until mid-afternoon, Union troops further south had been attempting to take the lower bridge across Antietam Creek. While some of his troops found places where the stream could easily be forded, the corps commander, General Ambrose Burnside, was determined to take the bridge that would eventually bear his name. It was defended by only 400 Confederate riflemen from Georgia and South Carolina. After four hours of fruitless attempts to capture the bridge, Federal troops from New York and Pennsylvania charged across and gained the west bank.

Throughout the morning, Lee had stripped his right of troops to support those hard pressed areas on his left and centre. Now, in spite of his slow progress, Burnside was in position to sweep the woefully inadequate Confederate defenders aside, capture Sharpsburg, and cut off the entire rebel army's avenue of retreat. He waited, however, for two precious hours, consolidating his hold on the west side of the creek. When Burnside finally got moving around 3.00 p.m., he made sluggish progress. An hour later, he was only

0.8km (0.5 mile) from the town. At the precise moment when he was needed the most, A.P. Hill and his Light Division appeared in a cloud of dust, bowling down the road from Harpers Ferry. His footsore soldiers had covered the 27.3km (17 miles) to the scene of the fighting in seven hours, and many had fallen out of the ranks due to exhaustion. The charge of the Light Division stopped Burnside's advance cold, and he retired toward the creek. By 6.00 p.m., the Battle of Antietam was over. Lee was too battered to take the offensive.

The casualties from America's bloodiest day were appalling. The Army of the Potomac counted 12,410 dead, wounded or missing, while the Army of Northern Virginia had lost 10,700. Throughout the day on 18 September, Lee stood his ground. McClellan declined to renew the fight and did not pursue the Confederate columns when they withdrew across the Potomac.

AFTERMATH

In the wake of the Battle of Antietam, President Lincoln became convinced that the outcome was enough of a victory to issue the Emancipation Proclamation, which freed the slaves in territory then in rebellion against the United States. The document transformed the war from an effort to save the Union to one of liberation and the perpetuation of freedom. European governments, which had abolished slavery themselves, were dissuaded from supporting the Confederate cause.

CONFEDERATE CAVALRYMAN

Armed with his trusty Colt revolver and wearing a jaunty uniform complete with a plumed slouch hat, the Confederate cavalryman was considered among the elite of his army.

ANTIETAM

UPPER BRIDGE

1 At dawn, Hooker's corps attacks Jackson on Lee's left flank. Thrust and counterthrust leave the cornfield and the Dunker Church grounds strewn with dead and wounded.

2 Mansfield assaults the Confederate left, making only limited progress, while Sedgwick's charging division of Sumner's corps plunges into Jackson's trap and is decimated.

DUNKER CHURCH

POTOMAC RIVER

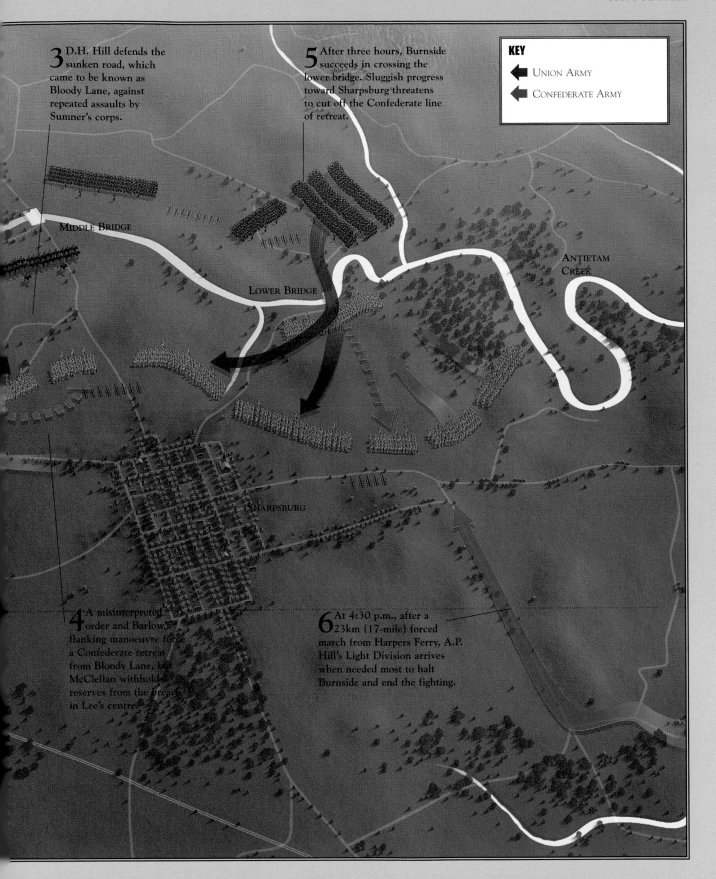

3 D.H. Hill defends the sunken road, which came to be known as Bloody Lane, against repeated assaults by Sumner's corps.

5 After three hours, Burnside succeeds in crossing the lower bridge. Sluggish progress toward Sharpsburg threatens to cut off the Confederate line of retreat.

KEY

⬅ UNION ARMY

⬅ CONFEDERATE ARMY

MIDDLE BRIDGE

ANTIETAM CREEK

LOWER BRIDGE

SHARPSBURG

4 A misinterpreted order and Barlow's flanking manoeuvre force a Confederate retreat from Bloody Lane, but McClellan withholds reserves from the breach in Lee's centre.

6 At 4:30 p.m., after a 23km (17-mile) forced march from Harpers Ferry, A.P. Hill's Light Division arrives when needed most to halt Burnside and end the fighting.

GETTYSBURG 1863

In an epic three-day battle, the brief history of the Confederacy reached its zenith as General Robert E. Lee's second invasion of the North was repulsed in southern Pennsylvania. After Gettysburg, the outcome of the American Civil War appeared inevitable as Union armies maintained an offensive posture on all fronts.

For General Robert E. Lee, the stunning Confederate victory at Chancellorsville in May 1863, provided both his crowning achievement and his darkest moment of battlefield command. Although the Union army under General Joseph Hooker had been routed, Lee's most capable lieutenant, General Thomas J. 'Stonewall' Jackson, had been mortally wounded by friendly fire. Although the loss of Jackson was a severe blow, Lee nevertheless felt compelled to follow up the victory at Chancellorsville. He reorganized the Army of Northern Virginia into three corps, commanded by generals James Longstreet, A.P. Hill, and Richard S. Ewell. The Confederate army was flush with victory and stood at the height of its strength;

GETTYSBURG FACTS

Who: General Robert E. Lee (1807–70) and 75,000 soldiers of the Confederate Army of Northern Virginia opposed 97,000 troops of the Union Army of the Potomac, commanded by General George G. Meade (1815–72).

What: During three days of fighting, Confederate forces failed to penetrate Union defences along a 4.8km (3 mile), fish hook-shaped line from Culp's Hill and Cemetery Hill southward along Cemetery Ridge to Little Round Top.

Where: South of the town of Gettysburg, in Southern Pennsylvania.

When: 1–3 July 1863.

Why: For the second time in the American Civil War, the Confederate Army launched an invasion of Northern territory.

Outcome: Lee's invasion was repulsed, and the military might of the Confederacy suffered irreplaceable losses in what was rapidly becoming a war of attrition. President Abraham Lincoln issued one of the enduring documents of American freedom with the Gettysburg Address.

IN THIS SECTION OF THE GETTYSBURG CYCLORAMA, *painted in 1883 by French artist Paul Philippoteaux, the 19th Massachusetts and 42nd New York regiments rush forward to bolster the Union line at the height of Pickett's Charge. During the high tide of Confederate military strength, a handful of the attackers breached the Union position on Cemetery Ridge, but only briefly.*

VERDUN

1916

Verdun epitomises the attritional struggle that became characteristic of the World War I on the Western Front. Intended to destroy the French reserves, the battle drew in massive numbers of German troops as well, and ended without any decisive result.

As World War I settled down into trench warfare in late 1914, it became more or less impossible to inflict a traditional victory on the enemy. Previously, victory was decided by the defeat of an army in the field or the occupation (or threat of occupation) of key areas such as capital cities. That was simply impossible now. There seemed to be no way to break through the lines and capture strategic objectives, and deep defensive positions made it virtually impossible to drive the enemy from the field. The problem in both cases was the availability of reserves, coupled with the capability to move them to a threatened point faster than a successful attack could be exploited.

Victory in the Great War would therefore be a matter of exhausting the other side, of making the cost of continuing so high that peace became essential, at

VERDUN FACTS

Who: French Second Army under General Henri Pétain (1856–1951), later replaced by General Robert Nivelle (1856–1924), versus the German Fifth Army under Crown Prince Wilhelm (1882–1951), with General Erich von Falkenhayn (1861–1922) with overall responsibility for operations as Chief of the General Staff.

What: The fortified city of Verdun was besieged and the attackers slowly ground their way in whilst artillery inflicted horrendous casualties. A counter-offensive eventually regained the lost ground.

Where: The city of Verdun on the Meuse river, France.

When: 21 February to 18 December 1916.

Why: The German high command wanted to draw French reserves into a 'meatgrinder' and destroy them, forcing France to make peace.

Outcome: After a hideous attritional struggle all that was achieved was massive casualties on both sides.

FRENCH INFANTRY ADVANCE through the shattered landscape, surrounded by the horrors of war. There is still something splendid about images of this sort – the reality was infinitely more dreary and squalid.

A FRENCH 1897-VINTAGE cannon. Designed for mobile operations in the open, weapons of this sort were less useful in the static trench warfare on the Western Front than high-trajectory howitzers and mortars.

whatever price. The key here, again, was reserves. So long as the opposition had sufficient manpower available to feed into the combat zone, the war could go on. The German high command therefore came up with a plan to destroy the French reserves by drawing them into a 'meatgrinder'. The German plan was to attack something that the French had to defend, and to destroy their army with artillery and infantry attacks. The chosen objective was the fortified city of Verdun.

VERDUN

Verdun was an ideal target in many ways. Lying in a loop of the Meuse river, the city had poor communications. Only one road ran in and out of the city. The logistic problems of the attack were eased by the fact that there was a major German railhead just 19.3km (12 miles) away, allowing quick transportation of ammunition, supplies and reinforcements as the attack developed. Verdun lay in a relatively quiet sector of the front, and many of the heavy guns of its forts had been sent to other sectors where they seemed to be more badly needed. It was garrisoned by three divisions, which represented fairly light defences.

German offensive plans included the assembly of 10 divisions to make the actual attack, supported by experimental 'infantry batteries' of 77mm (3in) field guns which were supposed to advance with the infantry to provide direct support but in the event were unable to cross the shell-torn wasteland. Another new weapon also made its debut at Verdun, the flamethrower. The attack was supported by large quantities of heavy guns – more than 1400 pieces in total. These included huge 420mm (16.5in) and 305mm (12in) weapons that had previously been used to reduce forts in Belgium. Over 500 minenwerfer were also deployed. These fired a 45.3kg (100lb) explosive shell which could have a deadly effect if it landed in a trench. Countless lighter weapons such as trench mortars were also available.

The offensive was codenamed Operation Gericht ('Judgement'). Its aim was to force the French into a battle of attrition on unequal terms. If they failed to meet the challenge, Verdun would fall. If they stood and fought, their army would be bled white and they would ultimately be forced to sue for peace. The operation was scheduled to start on 10 February, but was delayed by bad weather until the 21st. Although the preparations for the operation were spotted, there was no attempt to reinforce Verdun, and the initial artillery onslaught caught the garrison unprepared.

OPENING BARRAGE

As 21 February 1916 dawned, the frigid air was shattered by the scream of heavy shells and the 'whizz-bang' of anti-personnel weapons. Over two million shells fell on the forward French positions in the next 12 hours, after which the infantry began their attack. For the first two days the German forces made relatively little headway, but on the 24th they broke through the main defensive line, taking 10,000 prisoners and capturing 65 artillery pieces. The infantry were preceded in their attacks by a rolling barrage

A GERMAN FLAMETHROWER TEAM. Used to dig a determined foe out of good positions, early flamethrowers posed a threat to everyone around them, not just the enemy.

from the immense number of guns at their disposal, which wrecked the defences and drove the survivors under cover.

Between the awesome artillery barrage, the suddenness of the attack and the cold weather, the French were paralyzed. Some units broke and fled to the rear, leaving weak areas in the defences through which the German assault troops advanced. The whole Verdun defence was collapsing. Something had to be done, and fast.

Verdun was supposed to be invincible – a French army commission in 1915 had confirmed this, and sacked a general for saying otherwise. Yet on 25 February Fort Douaumont, a key component of the city's defences, fell to German assault. This was a serious blow to French morale, though it could have been avoided had the garrison not been stripped to the bone. The defending infantry had broken under bombardment leaving a platoon of artillerymen as the only defenders. A nine-man German patrol found a way into the fort and discovered that it was virtually undefended. They led 300 of their fellows in and captured the keystone of the Verdun defences almost without firing a shot.

PÉTAIN TAKES CHARGE

At the same time as Fort Douaumont was being captured by the enemy, General Pétain was arriving to take charge of the defences of Verdun. He found a desperate situation, with the only supply route into the city along a single road and a narrow-gauge railway alongside it. This road, dubbed La Voie Sacrée, was Verdun's inadequate lifeline, and Pétain's first task was to improve it. Thousands of men worked to widen the road, allowing a less restricted flow of supplies into the city. By the time they had finished, something like 6000 trucks could use the road every day, and over half a million troops, plus all their supplies, moved into and out of the city along it. Pétain decided that units were only to serve 15-day tours in the trenches, to allow them time to rest and recuperate, so La Voie Sacrée saw an endless stream of units rotating to and from the front line. Although Pétain had improved the desperate logistics situation, things were still bad. The fighting ebbed somewhat at the very end of February, only to be resumed on 5 March.

THE ATTACK IS RENEWED

A new German offensive was thrown in along the west bank of the Meuse, straight into the teeth of a well-prepared defence. Pétain had deployed his best troops to meet this assault, and they were supported by a powerful concentration of artillery. This assault marked something of a turning point in the defence of Verdun. French gunners were not only inflicting horrific casualties on the attackers, but were conducting effective counter-battery fire against their artillery. By the middle of April all the very heavy guns on the German side were out of action, and the German

GENERAL PHILIPPE PÉTAIN earned a hero's reputation at Verdun and later in the war but came to be considered a traitor for collaborating with the Nazis in World War II.

BELOW: FRENCH PRISONERS taken early in the Verdun offensive are escorted to the rear. Early German successes stunned the French into passivity and it was some time before the garrison began to fight back effectively.

artillery had suffered another serious blow when a shell landed among almost half a million heavy artillery shells stockpiled in Spincourt forest. This caused the largest single explosion of the entire war.

The attacks continued through April and into May, and threatened to indeed 'bleed the French army to death'. However, gains were relatively slight and when Pétain was relieved by General Robert Nivelle, the French began to recover their offensive spirit.

NIVELLE TAKES OVER

Where Pétain had been the defender of Verdun and had prevented its fall, Nivelle took the offensive. The French slogan for Verdun was 'Ils ne passeront pas!' ('They shall not pass!'), but Nivelle's aim was more than barring the door – he intended to kick the Germans back out. At first Nivelle could do no more than Pétain; German attacks were still making gains and with Fort Douaumont in German hands the crux of the defence was now Fort Vaux. Vaux protected an area of high ground from which German guns would be able to fire directly into the city and, even more importantly, at the bridges over which all supplies into the city were fed. Fort Vaux became the target of German assaults, and on 7 June it fell to them. Nevertheless, the balance was shifting. Nivelle was an artillery officer, and

THE GERMAN GEWEHR 98 was a fine rifle, but like all such weapons it was cumbersome in a close action such as a trench assault where fighting was hand-to-hand and shooting at very short ranges.

under his command the French guns became more effective. Even as the Germans advanced towards the surviving forts, Souville and Tavannes, their casualties mounted. Things hung in the balance throughout the end of June, and despite the opening of the Somme offensive on 1 July, the Germans pushed onwards, creeping ever closer to the city itself. On 11 July an attack actually reached Fort Souville, but its failure marked the end of German attempts to take Verdun. Thereafter they found themselves on the defensive as French counter-attacks began to retake some of the lost ground.

FRENCH COUNTER-ATTACKS

Nivelle's position was improved by the Somme offensive, which was launched partly to reduce the pressure on Verdun.

A REMARKABLY CLEAN and spruce German soldier poses with rifle and grenade. He wears a gas mask typical of the type issued later in the war. Early versions were hurriedly improvised and only marginally effective.

It did not succeed as an operation in its own right, but was successful in drawing in supplies and reinforcements that could otherwise be set against the defenders of Verdun. As the pressure eased, Nivelle launched counter-attacks to drive the Germans out and retake the lost forts. The largest of these was on 24 October, against Fort Douaumont and involved 170,000 infantry, 700 guns and over 150 aircraft. After this the French ground slowly forward, retaking Fort Vaux in early November. In mid-December the German army retreated from Verdun, leaving what was left of it in French hands.

'THE MEATGRINDER'

By the end of the Verdun offensive, the Germans had indeed managed to cause vast French casualties – 550,000 of them in fact. However, this was only achieved at a cost of 450,000 casualties of their own. During the summer it was obvious costly Somme offensive – which in turn cost both sides vast numbers of lives. In the end, what was a workable plan did not succeed and the battle was inconclusive. The German failure to take Verdun was a boost to morale on the Allied side, and although the Somme offensive failed to achieve anything significant either, the German army did pull back to the Hindenburg Line in 1917.

The vast casualties at Verdun and the Somme were partly to blame for the collapse of French morale in 1917, the increasing cynicism and mistrust of commanders among the British troops, and the decline of the German army, which lost the best of its junior leaders in the bitter fighting of 1916. Verdun was perhaps a situation where failure to win in an operational context paved the way for defeat at the grand strategic level.

that the cost was going to be very high, but the decision was taken to continue the offensive. One German casualty was the career of General Falkenhayn. On 29 August he was reassigned to command forces fighting against the Romanian army, which had joined the Allies the day before. This reassignment effectively represented a demotion. Falkenhayn was replaced by Hindenburg with Ludendorff as Quartermaster-General. Blaming Falkenhayn for the situation was perhaps unfair – he had realised as early as March that casualties were going to be too high, and pushed for an end to the operation. However, Crown Prince Wilhelm insisted on continuing.

The original German plan was reasonably sound – to attack something the enemy had to defend and drain his resources by artillery bombardment followed by infantry occupation of the devastated territory. However, the German army fell victim to 'mission creep', and at some point the capture of Verdun became the objective of the operation. This was not the plan originally – the idea was to destroy the French army, not to seize a city – and Verdun was not worth half a million troops.

However, as the battle went on the objective shifted until the German army was being ground down in order to take a city it did not want or need. Winning the battle had become more important than the strategic objectives that inspired it. This led to losses that could not be sustained and were wholly unnecessary.

AFTERMATH

Virtually every French division on the Western Front passed through the Verdun meatgrinder. Rather fewer, but still large, numbers of German formations were rotated into the offensive. Massive casualties on both sides reduced the fighting power and the morale of both forces, and arguably it was the plight of Verdun that forced the Allies to make their

FRENCH INFANTRY SERGEANT

There were no great differences between the equipment used by troops on both sides in World War I; this French sergeant's equipment is similar to that used by his German foes. A metal helmet offers some protection against overhead shell bursts and he is armed with a rifle and a bayonet. He may have a grenade or two available.

Although heavy artillery hurled tons of shells across the trench lines and specialist weapons gradually emerged including aircraft and armoured vehicles most of the great battles of the war were decided by infantrymen who doggedly clung to their positions or struggled to prise one another out of them.

of a siege, with heavily entrenched forces on both sides fighting from behind barbed-wire obstacles.

Between the big offensives, the war became one of raid and counter-raid, usually at night, with artillery pounding away at the opposing trenches. Infantry holding the forward positions were subjected to horrible conditions, huddling in their muddy dugouts and enduring bombardment whilst being unable to reply. Being under fire and unable to fight back is one of the most morally draining experiences men can suffer and morale was, unsurprisingly, a problem.

Something had to be done, for several reasons. The presence of German troops on Allied soil meant that it was not politically viable to sit on the defensive and hope that the naval blockade of Germany would eventually strangle her into submission. The French fortress of Verdun was at that time under pressure too. In short, the German army had to be attacked and defeated. It would be an expensive undertaking in terms of material and casualties, but in January 1916 when the plan was formulated the Allies believed that it could be done.

THE PLAN

The primary exponent of the plan was the French commander, Marshal Joseph Joffre (1852–1931). He wanted an offensive in the Somme area for the reasons listed above, and the British commander, General Sir Douglas Haig (1861–1928), was willing to consider it. Haig preferred the idea of an attack somewhere else, such as Flanders, where the terrain was better and there were more strategic objectives.

A BRITISH 11.75CM (4.7-IN) breech-loading gun. In the American Civil War, just 50 years previously, most artillery units were still armed with short-ranged smoothbore cannon. The increase in artillery killing power contributed to a static war.

He also wanted to wait for the reinforcements that the new conscription system would provide, and for fresh troops from around the Empire to arrive. There was also the possibility that the new secret weapon, codenamed 'tanks', might be some help. However, Joffre could not wait.

Haig proposed an assault in mid-August, but Joffre was adamant that the French army would not exist by then. He had originally proposed to use two French armies in the Somme offensive, but the Verdun meatgrinder reduced the French capabilities, and the original offer of 40 divisions was amended to 16. The remainder would have to come from the British. Nevertheless, the attack seemed to be practicable, and it was vital that something was done, so Haig agreed. The opening date for the offensive was set at 1 July 1916, and a force comprising 21 divisions was allocated to the initial offensive, with three infantry and five cavalry divisions in reserve to follow up a victory.

HEAVY DEFENCES

Although the Somme sector had been fairly quiet for some time, German defensive preparations had been continuous. The trenches were backed by strongpoints and dugouts in an impressive defensive complex that also included medical facilities, kitchens, laundries and electrical generating stations. Many of these installations were concealed by woods or villages, and their existence was not obvious to observers on the Allied side.

The Allies would have to cross low ground and fight their way uphill into the first line of German positions, which was overlooked by the second, and so forth. The defenders enjoyed an excellent view of the battlefield, making concealed preparations and manoeuvres very difficult. The defenders also had vast reserves of ammunition, and plenty of heavy weapons. Their high position also had psychological advantages whereas the Allied troops would be slogging uphill into the teeth of heavy resistance.

The Allied preparations for the offensive were not only observed from the enemy positions. Operational security was poor, and comments by British and French officers found their way into German intelligence reports. By the time the Allies opened up with their massive artillery bombardment on 24 June, the Germans already knew something was up. They had even guessed the date of the intended assault.

Although 1.75 million artillery shells were fired at German positions in a six-day preparatory bombardment, the defences were not seriously disrupted. Artillery fire was supposed to cut enemy wire, but all it tended to do was move it around and tangle it up even more. Muddy shell craters were tough going, and just to add to the misery heavy rain turned the whole area into a quagmire.

Although conscription had been introduced in Britain, most of the troops waiting to go over the top were in volunteer units from Kitchener's New Army. Among the attackers were several notable names – future military commanders Montgomery and Wavell, as well as Siegfried Sassoon and John Masefield.

On the German side the troops, who included an Austrian volunteer corporal named Adolf Hitler, were ready to receive and repel an assault. Casualties were taken, and a six-day bombardment, even ridden out in deep bunkers, is no joke. Overall, though, the defenders knew they were in good shape to deal with the coming attack. Their artillery was registered by map grid on the entire battlefield, and fire could be called down quickly on any enemy concentration.

The defenders could see the ground in front of their positions clearly, and were aware of choke points and obvious routes that attackers would be channelled into. Their machine guns were ready to sweep these areas as the enemy passed through them. If, somehow, the first trench line were taken, the defenders could fall back to secondary positions and carry on the fight from there.

THE FIRST DAY

The offensive began at 7.30 a.m. on 1 July, much as the Germans had predicted. All along the line, the attacking units lurched into motion, and the defenders began firing at them. The British forces went into action in long lines, proceeding at a walk across difficult terrain and stopping to struggle past tangles of wire. Initial reports to Haig were rather optimistic. At 8.00 a.m. he was to record that

THE GERMAN MAXIM 08 could spit death at a rate of 450 rounds per minute at a range of 2000m (6560ft). Its effectiveness as a defensive weapon was amply demonstrated at the Somme, when just a few guns were able to mow down whole British batallions in a matter of minutes.

THE BRITISH 'TOMMY'

At the battle of the Somme, each British soldier, or 'Tommy' as they were known, was covered in mud that dried in the sun and carried a formidable burden. Every soldier was carrying at least 27kg (60lbs) of equipment including a rifle with 220 rounds of ammunition, two hand grenades and a couple of (empty) sandbags to fortify captured enemy positions against counter-attack. In addition to this not inconsiderable load, many men carried other burdens. Everything that might be needed had to be transported forward by the assaulting troops. This included carrier pigeons, field telephones and their cables, digging equipment and extra ammunition. All of this had to be carried through mud and wire, uphill, under machine-gun fire.

everything was going well and the first enemy positions had been overrun. This was somewhat inaccurate. The reality was that British troops were being cut down in their thousands, often just beyond their trenches or in gaps in the wire that were becoming choked with bodies. Meanwhile, the French forces were also struggling. Their soldiers were less heavily burdened that the British and used more flexible tactics, rushing from position to position while others covered the advance with rifle fire. Although their

1ST JULY 1916: Preparing for the assault. Canadian troops fix bayonets as they await the order to go 'over the top'.

casualties were lighter (on account of not presenting such a wonderful target perhaps), the French force under General Fayolle did not have the numbers to smash a hole in the German lines.

HORRIFIC CASUALTIES

The first day of the Somme offensive resulted in some 57,470 British casualties, of whom almost 20,000 were killed. Only 585 were captured, mainly because few of the British troops got close enough to the German lines. Some units, such as the Canadian 1st Newfoundland Regiment, had been effectively wiped out. This horrific slaughter was made worse by the ponderous linear formation used by attacking units, although with such inexperienced troops there may have been no alternative.

The British had attacked with 200 battalions in 17 divisions of about 100,000 men. Of these, only five divisions got any men into the enemy positions at all. The rest were

halted in no-man's land. It was not for lack of trying, but the defenders were simply too strong. The Tyneside Irish Regiment, numbering about 3000 men, suffered nearly 100 per cent casualties. The regiment began its advance behind the main start line, in support of the initial attack. Despite the fact that this formation was not an immediate threat to the defenders, it came under such withering fire as it moved up that it never crossed the start line. A total of 500 men were killed or wounded in one battalion and 600 in another. Casualties might have been even higher, but for the fact that many defenders became so sickened by the slaughter that they ceased fire once the attackers in their sector stalled, and allowed the survivors to retreat unmolested.

ATTRITIONAL STRUGGLE

Despite the fact that fully 20 per cent of the attacking force had been killed, the Allies kept on attacking. Perhaps they had no alternative. Pressure had to be taken off Russia and Verdun somehow, and there was no time to build up for an offensive elsewhere. Logistics took too long, and the Allies needed to act now. Men could be fed in, but supplies and ammunition stocks took time to assemble. The Allies had to succeed on the Somme or at least pull in enough German reinforcements to reduce the pressure elsewhere.

At first the slaughter was very much one-sided as the Allies threw in new assaults and these were chewed up by the machine guns and artillery, or stalled on the wire. It may have seemed that the Allies were simply throwing away lives, and at first this may have been the case. For example, one German regiment took 180 casualties on the first day of the Somme whereas the British force facing it lost more than 25 times as many men.

For a fortnight little was achieved. Then, on 14 July a force of French and British troops managed to make some gains along the flanks of the Somme River. Minor gains followed, but the cost was immense, and fresh troops were fed into the battle on a regular basis as shattered formations had to be pulled out. Through July and August the slaughter went on, though now it was less one-sided. Forty-two German divisions were deployed to the Somme sector in those two months, and the necessity of counter-attacking Allied gains resulted in heavy casualties. At the end of July, casualties reached 200,000 for the Allies and 160,000 among German troops. The Allies had advanced 4.8km (3 miles), and little had changed at the end of August.

NEW IDEAS

Tactics had been evolving during the long struggle, and the raw British troops had learned from their more experienced French counterparts. Techniques like pre-dawn attacks had achieved some successes. The Allies were becoming more flexible and inventive. It was time to try something new. The

BARBED WIRE came in many different varieties, including the coiled 'Dannert' wire (far left), the virtually impenetrable high wire entanglements (centre left), and the apron fence, both square and pyramid shaped (right and far right). All sides sent out wiring parties at night to repair damage.

main problems facing the Allies were wire and machine guns, and now they, potentially, had a means to deal with both. Created specifically as a machine gun destroyer, the monstrous armoured fighting machine known as a 'tank' made its appearance. Tanks came in two types. 'Male' tanks mounted a main armament of 6-pounder guns derived from naval weapons, whilst 'female' tanks carried only machine guns. Both types were slow, prone to mechanical breakdown and required a large crew to operate. The could cross trenches, crush wire and, usually, shrug off small-arms and machine gun fire, which gave them a fighting chance.

Thirty-six tanks were deployed for a renewed assault, despite the fact that their crews were not fully trained. Only 18 went into action as the rest had broken down, but their appearance shocked the defenders into a panic. The Allies gained 3200m (3500 yards) for relatively slight cost, easily the biggest success of the offensive to date. However, it was not possible to exploit the breakthrough and several tanks were lost to artillery fire. The rest broke down or got stuck.

Tanks were not a decisive weapon on the Somme, mainly because they were committed in difficult terrain and in small numbers. Their success prompted further experiments, which were locally useful but achieved little on a strategic scale. That would change with the massed tank action at Cambrai in 1917, but for now the tank was simply another factor in a desperate struggle.

THE OFFENSIVE WINDS DOWN

As the weather worsened through October and November, the Allies attacked again and again, battering at the German positions until 19 November, when the operation was ceased. At that point the Allies had advanced no more than 11.2km (7 miles) along a 32.2km (20-mile) front. In mid-November, the casualty figures came to 419,654 for the British and 194,541 for the French, and this while the slaughter at Verdun was ongoing. These immense losses – just short of 615,000 – were sustained in failing to break through the Somme positions. However, the German army took 650,000 casualties in repelling the assault, and this had serious repercussions. The German army in 1914 was a splendid military instrument

'TANK TERROR' is the term used to describe the psychological effect of an armoured vehicle on infantry. Rifles and grenades were unlikely to halt even an early tank.

built on Prussian military traditions and victories in France and Austria. As 1917 began it was a tired and dispirited force whose best men had fallen in the struggles on the Somme. So many good young officers and NCOs had fallen that the German army never really recovered.

AFTERMATH

The Somme shook the confidence of the British army in its commanders and political leaders. It finished Joffre's military career, though Haig was promoted to Field Marshal at the end of the year. The battle is remembered as the worst slaughter in British military history, but in some ways it achieved its aims. The German army was badly battered and perhaps dismayed at the doggedness of the attackers. Whatever the reason, it fell back to the more easily defended Hindenburg Line in February 1917.

THE SOMME

2 The preparations are detected and German forces are ready to meet the onslaught. Despite a six-day artillery preparation, the initial assault is cut to pieces.

XIV (RES)

BOZERTIN -LE-PETIT

X

XX

III

XXX

38

FOURTH ARMY
RAWLINSON

ALBERT

XV

XIII

XXX

1 CAVALRY

MIRVOUS

2 INDIAN

3 With no alternative, British and French forces make repeated uphill attacks over the course of the next few weeks. These are bloodily repulsed.

BRAY

XXXXX

3 CAVALRY

GOUGH
(RESERVE)

SIXTH ARMY

PROVART

CORBIE

FAYOLLE

1 Needing to take the pressure off Verdun, the allies prepare a massive assault on the Somme.

XXXX

4 The availability of a handful of tanks makes a tactical success possible, but the gains are slight.

COMBLES

SECOND ARMY

VON BELOW

6 Although the Allies do not break through, they draw pressure off Verdun and inflict massive casualties. The German army later pulls back to better positions.

12 DIV

OLERY

PERONNE

XXX

XX

FLACOURT

I COLONIAL

121 DIV

5 The need to counter-attack draws in supplies and reinforcements destined elsewhere, and costs the German army heavily.

ATHIES

XXX

XX

XXXV

11 DIV

XXX

BOSIÈRES

KEY

◀	BRITISH FORCES
▨	BRITISH DIVISION
■	BRITISH CORPS
◥	BRITISH CAVALRY
◀	GERMAN FORCES
▨	GERMAN DIVISION
▬	GERMAN CORPS
◀	FRENCH FORCES
▬	FRENCH CORPS
————	JULY 1ST
··········	JULY 14TH
– – – –	SEPT. 15TH
–·–·–·–·	NOVEMBER

THE BATTLE OF BRITAIN 1940

In the summer of 1940, Britain was isolated on the fringe of a hostile continent. Only a narrow strip of water stood between British cities and the panzer divisions. Crossing 'the world's biggest anti-tank ditch' required air superiority, which ultimately the Luftwaffe failed to secure.

Some historians present the two World Wars as a single conflict with a 20-year ceasefire in between, and with hindsight it is not difficult to see how the roots of the second conflict lay in the first. In the 1920s, as a disarmed and humiliated Germany struggled with economic and social troubles, the rest of the world tried to come to terms with the cost of the recent Great War. Treaties were signed to limit naval construction and avoid a costly arms race, and the general feeling was that another war must be avoided at almost any cost.

THE BATTLE OF BRITAIN FACTS

Who: The German Luftwaffe versus the British Royal Air Force, augmented by foreign volunteers.

What: The German's attempts to destroy the RAF resulted in fierce air battles, which ultimately the Luftwaffe failed to win.

Where: British airspace, mainly over the southern and eastern counties.

When: Summer 1940.

Why: Hitler's Nazi Germany wanted to invade and subdue Britain, and needed air superiority to do so.

Outcome: A desperate struggle brought the RAF to the brink of defeat but ultimately it managed to hold on long enough to prevent invasion.

PILOTS OF NO. 92 SQUADRON Royal Air Force scramble for their fighters early on in 1941. The squadron took part in the final stages of the Battle of Britain, but by this time they had switched to offensive operations over France.

207

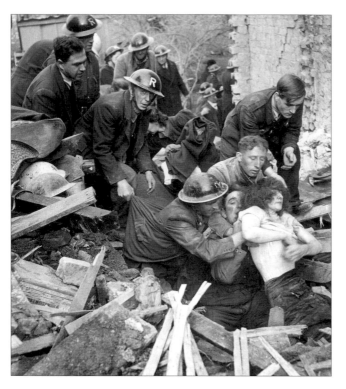

VICTIMS OF GERMAN BOMBERS are pulled from their homes in the East End of London by rescue workers during the Blitz.

As a consequence, Britain and her allies were completely unprepared to fight a second world war. The Royal Navy was substantial but was hampered by treaty limitations, while the army was small and under-equipped. In particular, armoured forces had not been developed with any real enthusiasm, despite the fact that the British invented armoured warfare.

THE ROYAL AIR FORCE

The Royal Air Force of the 1930s was something of a social institution, a private club for well-off young gentlemen who flew obsolescent aircraft and cut a dash at parties. Equipment was outdated, though entirely serviceable. Design and acquisition of new aircraft was of low priority. This could very well have cost Britain the war.

The Gloster Gladiator, the RAF's front-line fighter in 1937, was a very good aircraft in some ways – it was pilot-friendly, very manoeuvrable and had no vices – but it was a biplane fighter armed with four machine guns. The first production Messerschmitt Bf 109s were in service two years later, and had they met Gladiators over southern Britain the result would have been a massacre. Fortunately, a move in the late 1930s to develop a decent low-wing monoplane fighter for the RAF paid dividends, and just in time. The Gladiator was designed in the early 1930s, before air power

was really appreciated. Once it was realized that aircraft would play a major rule in any future war, new projects began to emerge.

The Hawker Hurricane was considered radical by many – 'eight machine guns is going a bit far' one critic claimed – but this was the armament carried by the Hurricane I, which first entered service in December 1937, and by September 1939 equipped 18 squadrons. The more famous Supermarine Spitfire entered service in August 1938, though in smaller numbers than the Hurricane. The Spitfire was originally also armed with eight 7.6mm (0.303in) machine guns, but a small number received 20mm(0.788in) cannon in place of four of the machine guns.

The decision to arm fighters with cannon or machine guns was influenced largely by their intended role. Multiple machine guns were considered best for defeating fighters, since a lot of bullets were required to obtain hits, and fighters were relatively fragile. Cannon were better for destroying bombers, since their heavier shells were more likely to cause serious damage to a large aircraft that could fly quite happily with a scattering of small holes in the fuselage. Many fighters adopted a hybrid armament of cannon and machine guns.

THE BOMBER THREAT

In Germany, which had created its air force from scratch in defiance of treaties forbidding it, there was no obsolete 'legacy' equipment to rely on, so modern aircraft had to be acquired from the outset. Thus German fighters and fighter-bombers were somewhat ahead of the competition. The disparity in equipment was not all that great, but there was a general feeling that the Hurricane was outmatched by the Bf 109 whereas the Spitfire was more or less its equal.

Air power had been very much in its infancy during World War I, but it had achieved very promising results. In the 1930s, it was thought that 'the bomber will always get through' and that bombing could achieve decisive results. Experience in the Spanish Civil War seemed to bear this out, and the effects of air raids on towns and cities were likely to be horrible. If a country were not to collapse and surrender due to civilian casualties, the bomber had to be stopped. Guns on the ground could do so much, but it was fighter interception that was the big hope in the fight against the bomber.

BRITISH PREPARATIONS

RAF Fighter Command fought hard during the Battle of Britain, of that there can be no question. However, it might not have prevailed but for the sophisticated detection and coordination system that supported it.

During the 1920s, the assumption in Britain was that the next great threat would come from the traditional enemy rather than a thoroughly defeated and demilitarized

Germany. In order to defeat the half-expected horde of French bombers, an early-warning system was set up in southern England. This consisted of acoustic detectors, effectively great stone mirrors that focussed sound at a single point and allowed aircraft to be heard at great distances – if they approached from the right direction.

The detectors themselves played no part in the Battle of Britain. However, the command and control system set up to feed their data to the fighter stations was still in place when war with Germany broke out in 1939. Its information came not from acoustic detectors but from the 'Chain Home' radar stations recently installed on the south coast. These stations provided early warning, which allowed a response to be planned and fitted to the circumstances. Had the fighters had to scramble when their pilots saw enemies overhead, the battle could not have been won.

THE OUTBREAK OF WAR

Things did not look good at the outbreak of war. After several months of 'phoney war' or 'Sitzkrieg', German forces advanced into France and overran its defences. The British were forced to refuse French requests for more Hurricane squadrons, effectively admitting that they did not think France could be saved.

The decision not to send fighters to reinforce defeat was a morally courageous one, and it played a part in the eventual salvation of all Europe from Nazism. The RAF was stretched thin enough as it was. Had more of its strength been sacrificed in a political gesture, Britain too might have been lost. Although the French, aided by British forces, put up a fight, they were simply unprepared for the armoured onslaught that they faced, and France was quickly knocked out of the war. Although much of the British army was evacuated and managed to reach home, it left behind most of its heavy equipment and needed time to reorganize and re-equip.

If Germany could launch the invasion of Britain (codenamed Operation 'Sealion') in the near future, the prospects of preventing it were slim. Various measures were put in place. Crash programmes to expand the army, backed up by a major fortification project and the formation of what became the Home Guard, offered a chance to resist an invasion. The navy declared that it could prevent an invasion for a time but not indefinitely. Its cruisers and

THIS LUFTWAFFE Heinkel He111 bomber pilot is wearing the one-piece canvas flying suit designed for summer use. He is also kitted out with a life-jacket, in case of the very real possibility of having to ditch his aircraft over the English Channel.

battleships could certainly shatter an invasion flotilla, but to do so they would have to operate in restricted waters under very hostile skies. The fleet was prepared to do what it could, but if the Germans had air supremacy then that amounted to going down fighting to buy time for the land forces.

Air supremacy was the key. With it, the German invasion would ultimately be unstoppable. Without it, the chances of success were much slimmer and so the Luftwaffe set out to secure control of the skies. Its commander, Reichsmarshall Hermann Göring (1893–1946), believed that the small and unprepared Royal Air Force would crumble quickly. He claimed that RAF Fighter Command could be put out of actions in four days, and after four weeks there would be nothing left of the British aircraft

MESSERSCHMITT BF 109

The Bf 109 was one of the best aircraft of its era, and its pilots accordingly held high status. Better than a Hurricane and only just matched by the Spitfire, the Bf 109 was a dangerous foe. Later in the war, it found itself outmatched by developed versions of existing Allied fighters and by aircraft designed specifically to beat it, but in the summer of 1940 the Bf 109 pilot was lord of the air and his machine almost without parallel. At various times the Bf 109 served as an air superiority fighter, an escort fighter, an interceptor, a ground-attack aircraft and a reconnaissance aircraft. The Bf 109 was produced in greater quantities than any other fighter aircraft in history, with over 31,000 units built.

THE MESSERSCHMITT BF 110 was a 'heavy fighter' intended to be able to escort bombers. It was outmatched by single-engined British fighters and was so badly mauled that the bomber escorts were sometimes given an escort of single-seaters.

fighting began on 30 June 1940. The raids were stepped up until, on 13 August, a major air offensive was launched against RAF airfields in the south of England. Adler Tag, 'Eagle Day', was a desperate time for Fighter Command. Aircraft that survived the fighting in the air might return to a bomb-cratered runway or be destroyed on the ground while rearming. Fighter Command was stretched to the limit, but it did not break. As ground crews rearmed and refuelled the undamaged planes, and

industry to produce replacement aircraft. This claim turned out to be somewhat optimistic.

THE BATTLE OPENS

Göring's plan was to draw out the RAF's fighter strength and destroy it by attacking targets such as coastal convoys, airfields and radar stations, as well as reducing Britain's capability to replace aircraft by bombing factories. The

did their best to return even badly shot-up ones to some semblance of serviceability, work parties filled in the runway craters while nearby soldiers manned machine guns and anti-aircraft guns to defend the embattled airfields.

Information came in from central command, directing the tired pilots to new battles as they took off again and again to intercept new raids. Particularly hit hard was 11 Group, which covered Kent and Sussex, but somehow they managed to go on fighting through 'Eagle Day' and the terrible weeks that followed. The projected four days were long gone, and yet the RAF was still in the fight. At times reeling like a punch-drunk boxer who just will not go down, Fighter Command fought back with everything at its disposal, and each raid bled the Luftwaffe.

The British enjoyed a number of advantages over the attackers, though it might not have seemed like it at the time. British aircraft entered battle close to home, benefiting from the traditional advantage of 'interior lines' over an enemy who had to travel to the battlefield. Thus fighters could be switched from one target to another as long as they had fuel and ammunition, and as long as their pilots could stand it. Fighting at a distance from its airfields took its toll on the Luftwaffe. Pilots were required to spend more time in unproductive travel to and from the battle area, which wasted fuel, increased maintenance requirements per minute of combat time, tired out pilots and also took aircraft out of the fight for much longer than their British equivalents, which were often fighting over their own bases.

Of course, this did mean that German pilots had less combat time per day while RAF men were flung from one action to the next with

ONE OF THE FINEST FIGHTERS of all time, the Supermarine Spitfire served in 40 different versions. It was slightly faster and much more manoeuvrable than the Bf 109, but it could be out-climbed by its foe.

a corresponding psychological effect. The RAF was also reinforced throughout the battle by foreign volunteers and newly-trained pilots. The foreigners included Free Polish, French and Scandinavian pilots plus New Zealanders, South Africans, Canadians and even American citizens who had come to fight alongside the British even though their nation was not yet at war with Germany.

All the same, 'The Few' were getting fewer and the battle was far from won. The decision to commit fresh squadrons from less heavily beset northern sectors resulted in a massacre. These green pilots were flung into intense battle against an enemy with far more experience. Those that survived learned fast and were soon giving as good as they got.

SWITCHING TARGETS

From the German perspective, the failure of the RAF to roll over and die was inexplicable. Surely nobody could stand such horrific combat for so long and keep fighting? Göring was very jealous of the prestige of his Luftwaffe, and had staked its reputation on beating the RAF. So why wouldn't the RAF give up? In fact, Fighter Command was at the end of its tether. There were times when every flyable aircraft was in the air, and even then there were too few of them.

Perhaps not realizing that the RAF was, indeed, being ground down, Göring ordered a change in strategy. A German bomber had missed its industrial target and hit a residential area of London, and RAF Bomber Command had retaliated with a raid on Berlin. Hitler was incensed, and so deliberate attacks on London and other cities were ordered. Fighter Command had to respond to the bombing raids, but the RAF was no longer the main target. Now that its airfields were no longer under direct attack, the strain lessened slightly and hopes began to rise. Fighter Command began to grow in strength and in time gained the upper hand. It had come very close to extinction but clung on long enough to ensure victory.

VICTORY

Unlike a land battle, it is hard to determine a clear point where one side had won and the other lost in the Battle of Britain. Things certainly looked bleak for Britain on 15 September, but on the 17th Hitler decided that the invasion of Britain was not possible and cancelled Operation 'Sealion'. It can be reasonably claimed that the Battle of Britain was not so won as such by the British; it was more that the Luftwaffe failed to achieve victory.

This nonetheless represented a strategic victory for the British – the Battle of Britain was fought to prevent an invasion by German forces – even though there was no clear moment where tactical victory was achieved. While there is some doubt that the invasion would have been successful, the fact remains that it was cancelled because the RAF was

still holding out despite everything the Luftwaffe could do to it. Churchill referred to the pilots of RAF Fighter Command as 'the Few', and rightly commented that a very great deal was owed to these heroes. But let us not forget the other architects of victory. Those who pushed for good, modern fighter aircraft just in time, those who repaired, refuelled and rearmed the fighters, who filled in the craters and defended the airbases while they themselves were under attack, and the unsung coordinators who gathered radar data and turned it into successful interceptions. Victory in the Battle of Britain was a team effort. It was won by tenacity in the face of tremendous odds, and it most likely changed the course of the war.

AFTERMATH

The battle to destroy the RAF cost the Luftwaffe 1733 aircraft. The RAF lost 915. Some British pilots were shot down several times. There are documented cases of men crashing near their base, running to the nearest aircraft and going up again. Against such fighting spirit it is not hard to see how the Luftwaffe failed to win.

There was no sudden end to the air attacks, which continued throughout the war. London and other cities were bombed many times and there were plenty of smaller raids on factories and shipping to which Fighter Command responded. But from 17 September 1940 onwards the threat of invasion receded. In 1941 Hitler sealed his fate by ignoring a bloody, battered but undefeated Britain on his flank and invading the Soviet Union. Later that year the USA entered the war. On 6 June 1944 British, US and Canadian troops landed in France to begin the liberation of Europe. They landed from the south of England, from territory kept free of enemies by the courage and skill of a few fighter pilots.

AN RAF PILOT MID-SCRAMBLE. Initially commissioned officer-pilots and enlisted sergeant-pilots were segregated and had different messes although they fought together. The Battle of Britain did much to bring equality among 'The Few'.

THE BATTLE OF BRITAIN

4 The shattered southern fighter groups are reinforced from northern sectors. There are no reserves left now, but after horrific initial losses these new pilots quickly become veterans.

FIGHTER COMMAND
13 GROUP

FIGHTER COMMAND
12 GROUP

2 The battle escalates as the Luftwaffe directly attacks RAF fighter airfields and aircraft factories. Fighter Command is ground down but fights back.

FIGHTER COMMAND
10 GROUP

6 The RAF gradually builds up its strength until its survival is no longer in doubt. The Luftwaffe has failed to win the Battle of Britain, though this is not immediately apparent.

LUFTFLOTTE 5
(FROM NORWAY)

KEY

RAF AIR BASES

MAIN ANTI-AIRCRAFT BATTERIES

LUFTWAFFE AIR BASES

RADAR STATIONS

LUFTWAFFE ATTACKS

HIGH-LEVEL RADAR

LOW-LEVEL RADAR

1 The battle opens with raids designed to draw out British fighter strength to be destroyed. Coastal installations and shipping are among the targets.

London

FIGHTER COMMAND
11 GROUP

LUFTFLOTTE 2

3 Although the RAF is at this point essentially beaten, its pilots keep on fighting anyway. The Luftwaffe takes punishing losses in a roughly two-for-one exchange.

LUFTFLOTTE 3

5 Frustrated at their inability to break the RAF, Göring and Hitler order a switch of targets, relieving pressure on Fighter Command.

Paris

STALINGRAD 1942

The turning point of World War II, the battle of Stalingrad was a savage and bitter urban conflict in which tens of thousands of German and Soviet troops were killed. It was here that the Red Army proved it could not only hold off the Wehrmacht in a defensive battle, but also take the offensive and defeat the seemingly invincible German war machine.

Operation 'Barbarossa', the German invasion of the Soviet Union, was the largest land invasion in history, pitting 3.6 million German troops and their allies against some three million Soviet troops in the western Soviet Union. Tactically and doctrinally superior, the Germans advanced further and faster than any other modern army, capturing some three million prisoners in the process. Yet the Soviet Union did not collapse as Hitler had so confidently predicted. Unclear strategic goals, logistical overstretch, unexpectedly tough Soviet resistance and the terrible Russian winter meant that the Germans failed to defeat their enemy decisively in 1941. Indeed the Red Army was able to launch a counter-offensive at Moscow on 5–6 December,

STALINGRAD FACTS

Who: The German Sixth Army under General Friedrich Paulus (1890–1957) against the Soviet Sixty-Second Army under General Vasily Chuikov (1900–82).

What: The Germans, bogged down in urban fighting where their superior mobile tactics were useless, were unable to take the city and were subsequently trapped by the Soviet counter-offensive and the Sixth Army surrendered.

Where: The city of Stalingrad on the Volga River, in the southern Soviet Union.

When: 14 September 1942 to 2 February 1943.

Why: The Germans sought to take

Stalingrad to deal both a material and psychological blow to further Soviet resistance.

Outcome: Stalingrad was the turning point in the war on the Eastern Front, when the Soviets won their first major victory.

A GERMAN MORTAR DETACHMENT prepares to move in the factory district of the city. Some of the fiercest fighting occurred around the factories, and the Red October factory was never captured in its entirety, despite numerous attacks.

GERMAN INFANTRY MANHANDLE *a light infantry gun into position during the fighting in the north of Stalngrad. Light guns were often used against defended infantry positions.*

which caught the over-extended, exhausted Germans unawares, pushing them back over 160km (100 miles) in places before the line stabilized.

'Barbarossa' had cost the German army 1.1 million casualties. Only eight of the Eastern Army's 162 divisions were at full strength. Losses of vehicles were similarly high. By the spring of 1942 there was no question of resuming the offensive along the whole front, rather the Germans only had the resources for a single thrust. Stalin and the Soviet High Command anticipated that the Germans would resume their assault on Moscow and therefore massed their reserves in the area.

However, with the entry of the USA into the war in December 1941, Germany was now faced with the prospect of the opening of a Second Front and a long war of attrition. Thus Hitler decided to drive south toward the Transcaucasus and the oil fields which supplied 90 per cent of Soviet fuel. In the short term this would deny the Soviets fuel and in the long term provide resources for a drawn-out war against Britain and the USA. He set out this view in Führer Directive No 41 on 5 April 1942, stating that: 'All available forces will be concentrated on the main operations in the Southern sector, with the aim of destroying the enemy before the Don, in order to secure the Caucasian oil fields and the passes through the Caucasian mountains themselves.'

OPERATION 'BLUE'

Operation 'Blue', as the plan was code-named, was undertaken by Army Group South consisting of one million German and 300,000 allied troops, supported by *Luftflotte* 4 with 1500 aircraft. There were two main axes of advance; Army Group A would drive for the Caucasus, while Army Group B would secure the northeastern flank of the advance along the Don and Volga Rivers. 'Blue' opened on 28 June 1942 and initially the Germans made rapid advances. Although they managed to inflict a number of telling defeats on the Soviets, Stalin had given permission to the Red Army to trade space for time and the retreat was made in reasonably good order.

Army Group A reached the oil fields at Maikop on 9 August, but the advance slowed thereafter as resources were switched to Army Group B. Its main formation was Sixth Army commanded by Colonel-General Friedrich Paulus, which was pushing toward the city of Stalingrad, which sat on the major crossing point of the Volga River. On 23 July, Hitler ordered that the city be taken. Militarily there were some sound reasons for capturing Stalingrad, as it would secure the flank of Army Group South and block an obvious launching point for a Soviet counter-attack. However, the main motivations were political and psychological. The capture of the city that bore Stalin's name would be of huge value to the morale of both Germany and its allies.

STALINGRAD

Stalin also understood the importance of the city. On 12 July he established the Stalingrad Front made up of the Sixty-Second, Sixty-Third and Sixty-Fourth Armies. A week later the city itself was put on an immediate war footing, but there was to be no mass evacuation of the population as Stalin believed that the troops would fight better for a 'living city'. On 23 July he issued Order No 227 that the Red Army would take 'Not a step back'. German commanders noticed a definite stiffening of Soviet resistance, but they were able to batter their way through Sixty-Fourth Army and cross the Don on 23 August.

The same day *Luftflotte* 4 launched a massive air raid on Stalingrad causing 30,000 casualties. The first German spearheads reached the Volga at Rynok and entered Stalingrad's northern suburbs. However, the advance on the city slowed in the face of poor terrain and desperate Soviet resistance. Thus the bulk of Paulus' army only reached the outskirts of central Stalingrad in early September. Herman Hoth's Fourth Panzer Army suffered similar difficulties in reaching the southern suburbs around about the same time.

THE OPPOSING FORCES

The Soviets estimated that about 170,000 men, 500 tanks and 3000 artillery pieces faced them on the 64.3km (40-mile) front around Stalingrad and its environs. They themselves could muster about 90,000 troops, 120 tanks and 2000 guns. A similar imbalance faced the defenders on the narrower front of the city itself, with the defending 54,000 strong Sixty-Second Army up against about 100,000 Germans. These numbers fluctuated through out the battle due to losses and reinforcement, but the force ratios remained reasonably constant throughout. The main commanders were Paulus, an excellent staff officer and a capable solider, but probably unsuited to the bitter, attritional and messy urban battle which confronted him. Vasily Chuikov, commanding Sixty-Second Army, could not have contrasted more with the neat, fastidious Paulus. Tough, earthy and bloody-minded, he was just the man for the grim task ahead of him and his troops.

Chuikov had also thought hard about how he was going to beat his adversary. The Soviets had chosen their ground well. In the campaigns that preceded Stalingrad, the Soviets had proved tactically and operationally inferior in the

TWO GERMAN SENIOR NCOS take a shelter in a bomb crater in the initial fighting to capture the suburbs of Stalingrad. Both men are armed with MP38s, ideal weapons for close-quarter fighting in a built-up environment.

RED ARMY SOLDIER

This Red Army rifleman is wearing the new pattern winter uniform introduced in 1941. By late 1942, his *telogreika*, a padded khaki jacket, was in common usage throughout the Red Army. He wears the matching padded trousers, *valenki* felt boots and the so-called 'fish-fur' cap or *shapka-ushank*, because the material it was manufactured from bore very little relation to real fur. He is armed with a PPSh-41 submachine gun. Ideal for urban warfare, the compact, robust PPSh-41 made up a large proportion of Soviet infantry weapons during the Battle of Stalingrad.

manoeuvre warfare that characterized the fighting on the wide-open spaces of the steppes. Key to German success had been the coordination of their infantry and armour and particularly close air support. They had, up to this point, eschewed urban combat in major conurbations. However, military and particularly political necessity meant the Germans would be fighting in an environment where their skills in manoeuvre were irrelevant. Even more importantly, their close air support would be considerably less effective. Conversely the Soviets' proven defensive tenacity, skill in close combat and willingness to take losses would be a considerable advantage.

THE MAMAYEV KURGAN

The Germans' first attempt to take the city opened on 14 September with a two-pronged assault by LI Corps on the centre and south, supported by a push from the extreme southern suburbs by Fourth Panzer Army. The aim was to seize the dominating heights of the Mamayev Kurgan, where Chuikov had his headquarters, and capture the central landing stage, splitting the Sixty-Second Army in two and isolating it from resupply. An artillery strike knocked out Chuikov's HQ and the Germans pushed up over the

IN AN OBVIOUSLY STAGED PROPOGANDA photograph, a group of Soviet soldiers move cautiously through the ruins of Stalingrad amidst the fighting during the Autumn of 1942. All are armed with Soviet PPSh-41 submachine guns.

Mamayev Kurgan towards Stalingrad No 1 railway station and the landing stages on the Volga River. Chuikov committed his last tactical reserves and pleaded with his Front commander, Colonel-General Yeremenko, to send him Major-General Rodmitstev's elite 13th Guards Division. The division had to fight its way from the landing stage to the station and on to the southeastern slopes of the Mamayev Kurgan. The station changed hands 15 times with the German 71st Division finally securing it on 19 September. By then the 13th Guards, which had entered the battle 10,000 strong could muster just 2700 men.

In the south of the city, the Fourth Panzer Army met intense resistance, culminating in the battle around the grain silo, where fifty naval infantry and guardsmen held up three German divisions for several days. However, by 26 September Fourth Panzer Army had reached the Volga and split Sixty-Fourth Army from Chuikov's Sixty-Second Army. The Sixth Army held the crest of Mamayev Kurgan and made substantial gains in the centre. Paulus could declare that 'the battle flag of the Reich flies over the Stalingrad Party building', but the battle was far from over.

THE VOLGA CROSSINGS

Although the fighting continued around Mamayev Kurgan, the main German effort shifted into the factory district on 27 September. The German attacks against the Soviet positions based around the industrial complexes of the Red October, Barrikady and the Tractor factories, were intended to capture the landing stages behind them. Controlling the Volga was the key to the battle, as it was Sixty-Second Army's vital lifeline. Despite the tactical dominance of the Luftwaffe and the best efforts of the German artillery, they never managed to stop the flow of supplies and men across the river. After a week of bitter fighting the Sixth Army managed to cut off the Tractor Factory.

There was a lull in fighting and then the Germans redoubled their efforts in the factory district, finally capturing Barrikady and most of Red October. By the end of October they held 90 per cent of the city and had all the Soviet-controlled areas under fire. But this had only been achieved at a massive cost. The Sixth Army was battered and exhausted and still it was not enough. The Red Army had taken the best the Wehrmacht could throw at and still clung onto the banks of the Volga. On 11 November, Paulus launched his last major assault, again in the factory district. It met with some success as German troops managed to reach the west bank of the river.

THE SOVIET-MADE MOSIN NAGANT M1891/30 was considered one of the best-made rifles of World War II. It was prized by both ordinary soldiers and specialists, such as snipers, who used it to great effect at Stalingrad.

ZHUKHOV'S COUNTER-ATTACK

To maintain momentum over the seven weeks of bitter house-to-house fighting, the German command reduced the length of front held by Sixth Army and Fourth Panzer Army, leaving the flanks covered by Italian and Romanian forces. Stalin had given General Georgi Zhukhov (1896–1974) the task of organizing a counter-attack to cut off the Sixth Army in Stalingrad. He built up one million men and 900 tanks in the hinterland behind the Volga, undetected by the Germans. Zhukov launched his assault, Operation 'Uranus', on 19 November. Three Armies of General Vatutin's South-West Front smashed through the Third Romanian Army and a day later Yeremenko's Stalingrad Front brushed aside the Fourth Romanian Army in the south. The two fronts met at Kalach on 23 November, completing a perfect encirclement, that trapped roughly 250,000 German and Axis troops in the Stalingrad pocket.

Paulus requested permission to break out, but Hitler refused. The head of the Luftwaffe, Herman Göring, pledged to supply the Sixth Army by air and Hitler ordered Field Marshal von Manstein (1887–1973) to prepare a counter-attack to relieve Paulus' trapped troops. Operation 'Winter Storm', which opened on 12 December, needed to cover about 97km (60 miles). It was stopped 59km (35 miles) south of Stalingrad. Meanwhile Zhukov launched his offensive code-named 'Little Saturn', threatening the entire German position in the south. 'Winter Storm' was the Sixth Army's last hope. The Luftwaffe barely managed to land a third of the

supplies required and from 10 January the German position was increasingly constricted by Operation 'Ring', General Rokossovsky's Don Front and his attempt to close the pocket. Despite the futility of the struggle, the Soviets were impressed by the resilience of the German defenders. Nonetheless, they took about half the pocket in a week and after the last airfield fell, Paulus asked Hitler for permission to surrender. He was refused. By 29 January the Germans had been reduced to two pockets in city, one around the Unimag Department Store in the centre, the other in the factory district. On 31 January Hitler promoted Paulus to Field Marshal. The implications were obvious; no German commander of that rank had ever been captured alive. But Paulus surrendered that day; the northern pocket held out until 2 February. German casualties at Stalingrad were about 200,000, with 110,000 of the Sixth Army going into Soviet captivity. Only 5000 ever made it home.

AFTERMATH

Stalingrad marked a decisive turn in the war against Germany. The Soviet Army had outfought and out-thought the Wehrmacht. Although Germany would maintain a tactical edge, at Stalingrad, the Soviets demonstrated a superior grasp of the operational and strategic level of war. The Red Army had drawn the Wehrmacht into an attritional battle. Yet it had also been able launch a large-scale, mobile 'manoeuvrist' operation that encircled and destroyed the Sixth Army. The victory at Stalingrad would be followed by many more.

THE STURMGESCHÜTZ III ASSAULT GUN was an important part of German offensive operations at Stalingrad. These turretless armoured vehicles provided the assaulting German infantry with crucial support with direct fire on point targets, such as machine-gun emplacements and heavily defended buildings.

STALINGRAD

RYNOK

16 PZ

60 MOT

DZERSHINSKY
TRACTOR FACTORY

BARRIKADY FACTORY

5 Throughout October the Germans maintain their pressure in the factory district, bringing 90 per cent of the city under their control.

388

100

3 On 27 September the Germans shift their main effort into the factory district in an attempt to capture the landing stages behind them.

295

1 The German LI Corps launches its first assault on the city on 14 September in an attempt to capture Mamayev Kurgan and the central landing stage by the river.

KEY

← GERMAN MOVEMENT

GERMAN INFANTRY DIVISION

GERMAN ARMOURED DIVISION

GERMAN MOTORIZED DIVISION

6 The last major German attack begins on 11 November. Eight days later the Soviets launch Operation 'Uranus', cutting off the Sixth Army in the city.

4 The Soviets managed to maintain their supply lines across the Volga, providing the 62nd Army with just enough men and material to hang on to their foothold in the city.

RED OCTOBER FACTORY

62ND ARMY HQ

KRASNAYA SLOBODA

MAMAYEV KURGA

PAVLOV'S HOUSE

NKVD HQ

NO. 1 RAILWAY STATION

GRAIN SILO

RIVER VOLGA

2 The Fourth Panzer Army attacks in support in the south of the city, but are held up by fanatical resistance around the grain silo.

MIDWAY 1942

The turning point of the Pacific War, the battle of Midway saw US carrier aircraft destroy the Japanese carriers that had attacked Pearl Harbor. Thanks to signals intelligence and good luck, a Japanese plan to lure the American carriers into a trap instead spelled the end of Japanese naval dominance of the Pacific.

Japan's surprise strike on Pearl Harbor on 7 December 1941 had been a remarkable tactical success, but because the American aircraft carriers had been out to sea, it had been an incomplete victory. One of those aircraft carriers, the *Hornet*, took 16 B-25 bombers to attack Tokyo and Nagoya, inflicting little serious damage, but providing the Americans with a major morale boost in what became known as the 'Doolittle Raid'. In May, the Americans again used their carriers to check Japanese moves toward Australia at the Battle of the Coral Sea. These two incidents led senior Japanese leaders to conclude that they had to eliminate the remaining American carriers in order to provide Japan with strategic space. Time was crucial because the

MIDWAY FACTS

Who: A Japanese armada of four aircraft carriers carrying 256 aircraft, 11 battleships and numerous smaller vessels opposed an American force that included three aircraft carriers, 234 carrier- and land-based planes, and a variety of smaller craft.

What: American carrier-based aircraft attacked and destroyed Japan's aircraft carriers, thus removing Japan's long-range strike and scouting capabilities.

Where: In the Pacific Ocean, northwest of Midway Island.

When: 3–6 June 1942.

Why: The Japanese had hoped to seize Midway Island as an advance base and as a

means to lure the American fleet into a decisive battle.

Outcome: The United States destroyed Japan's aircraft carriers, giving the Americans an advantage in the Pacific War that proved to be crucial.

US NAVY PERSONNEL *from a damaged ship are hauled out of the sea by comrades at the Battle of Midway. American losses at Midway were minor compared to the Japanese, and included one carrier, one destroyer, 150 aircraft and 307 men.*

United States was then in the process of converting its massive industrial potential into a military asset that the Japanese knew they could not hope to match.

JAPANESE PLANS

The Japanese Admiral Isoroku Yamamoto (1884–1943), architect of the Pearl Harbor strike, sought to lure the Americans into a carrier fight that he expected his more experienced sailors and airmen to win. A Japanese capture of Midway Island, he predicted, would force the Americans to come to battle on terms advantageous to the Japanese. Once the American fleet had been crushed, Japan could then convert Midway into a major airbase and a safe place from which to monitor American actions in Hawaii. The erroneous report of the sinking of the *Yorktown* at the Battle of the Coral Sea gave the Japanese even more confidence that they had the American fleet outgunned and outclassed. The Japanese navy spared nothing to make Midway a success, assembling approximately 200 ships, including 11 battleships, eight carriers, 23 cruisers, 65 destroyers and

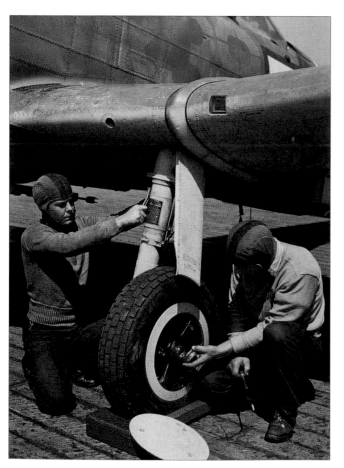

BROUGHT INTO SERVICE *the year before Midway, the Dauntless SBD Dive Bombers were critical to American victory. This photo shows the underrated American repair crews who kept the planes flying and the ships at sea.*

20 submarines. This force represented the vast majority of the Japanese fleet. The Japanese admirals confidently expected this massive armada to dispatch any American force sent out to meet it.

Partly because of his overconfidence in Japan's material (and presumably moral) superiority, Yamamoto made the fateful decision to divide his forces. He sent a diversionary force that included four battleships and two cruisers north toward the western Aleutian Islands in Alaska. These ships played no role in the battle and, as events turned out, also failed to lure any American ships into taking the bait. The main force, itself the largest armada in the history of the Pacific Ocean, was also split.

Submarines moved ahead of the main Japanese forces to find the location of the American ships, report those positions, then prepare to join the battle. The van, or main strike force, commanded by the able Admiral Chuichi Nagumo (1887–1944), included four powerful aircraft carriers: the *Kaga*, carrying 30 fighters, 23 bombers and 30 torpedo bombers; and the *Hiryu*, *Soryu* and *Akagi*, each carrying 21 fighters, 21 bombers and 21 torpedo bombers. The van also included battleships, cruisers and destroyers to protect the carriers. The final part of the Japanese force was the Midway landing force of surface ships and troop transports.

AMERICAN MOVES

Two major feats by the Americans greatly undermined Japanese preparations. Lieutenant Commander James Rochefort, an eccentric cryptologist who was more comfortable in his bathrobe than his Navy uniform, had broken enough of the Japanese naval code to guess the general lines of the Japanese plan. Rochefort had intercepted and decrypted plans for a major Japanese operation against a target codenamed 'AF'. Rochefort's instincts told him that 'AF' had to be Midway, but American naval commander Admiral Chester W Nimitz (1885–1966) still feared that 'AF' might be Oahu. To make sure, Rochefort designed a clever ruse. He sent out an unencoded message over a frequency he knew the Japanese were monitoring, stating that Midway's fresh water system was not working properly. A few days later, when he saw a decoded Japanese order for tanks of fresh water to accompany the 'AF' operation, he had the confirmation he and Nimitz needed. Now American naval assets could be concentrated on Midway without jeopardizing the safety of Oahu.

The other great American success involved the carrier *Yorktown*. Damaged so badly at the Coral Sea that Japanese pilots reported her sunk, the *Yorktown* had limped back to Pearl Harbor, where repair crews worked furiously over the course of just three days to get her ready in time to sail towards Midway with Rear Admiral Frank Jack Fletcher's

LEFT: THE GRUMMAN F4F-3 'Wildcat' was the mainstay of the US Navy's carrier aircraft in the first year of the war. Nearly 8000 Wildcats were built over the course of the war, and they featured prominently at Pearl Harbor, Coral Sea and Wake Island, as well as the crucial Battle of Midway.

RIGHT: THE UBIQUITOUS Mitsubishi 'Zero' initially offered a shock to the Allies in the Pacific theatre, outclassing all opposing Allied aircraft. This is the A6M3 model, which came into service in 1942, and could be used as a dive-bomber and fighter.

Task Force 17 on 30 May 1942. The Yorktown was in a far from ideal condition, but her aircraft were unaccounted for in Japanese plans. Both Task Force 17 and Rear Admiral Raymond Spruance's Task Force 16 left Pearl Harbor before the Japanese submarines could get into position. Thus not only did the Americans have an aircraft carrier unknown to the Japanese, the Japanese had no reliable information on the whereabouts of the American ships.

Thanks in large part to Rochefort's efforts, the United States Navy did not fall for the Aleutian decoy. With the damaged but serviceable *Yorktown*, the Navy could count on three carriers, including the *Enterprise*, and the *Hornet*. The Americans could also count on the assistance of land-based planes on Midway Island itself. The Americans had a total of 233 carrier- and 127 land-based aircraft to meet the 248 planes of the Japanese force. The United States, still recovering from the losses at Pearl Harbor, had nothing to counter Yamamoto's seven battleships, but it was now in a position to fight the battle using carriers at long range, thus leaving the battleships isolated. As at Coral Sea, the entire battle was fought by planes from carriers; the surface ships never even saw one another, owing to the great range of the carrier aircraft.

THE FIRST STRIKE

Unbeknownst to the Japanese, then, the Americans had a reasonably useful idea of what to look for and where to spot it. Just after midnight on 4 June 1942, American patrol planes spotted the Japanese van less than 965km (600 miles) from Midway Island. Although American attempts to inflict damage on the Japanese fleet from the air failed, the early warning allowed Midway to prepare its defences and its aircraft. For his part, Admiral Nagumo was undeterred by

what he understood as a fluke American overflight of his carriers. Accordingly, he launched his air attack of 108 planes against Midway at 4.30 a.m. when his ships were still 386km (240 miles) away from Midway. The Americans, ready

JAPANESE SAILOR

The Imperial Japanese Navy (IJN) in 1942 was a powerful force with a history of big victories. Since the Russo-Japanese War of 1904–05 the Navy had seen a string of successes and a steady rise in importance. More recently, in addition to Pearl Harbor, the Japanese could look with pride on their technical abilities in the Singapore and Philippines campaigns. Its sailors were confident, disciplined and aggressive. Service in the IJN came with great prestige; consequently, 80 per cent of Japanese sailors were volunteers, a much higher percentage than Japanese soldiers. Japanese sailors especially excelled at gunnery, navigation and night fighting. Specially trained Japanese sailors supported amphibious warfare and naval aviation, the two branches the IJN most heavily relied on during their planning for Midway.

LEFT: ADMIRAL CHESTER W. NIMITZ *became the Commander of the Pacific Fleet after Pearl Harbor. Aggressive and willing to take risks, he played decisive roles in the American victories at the Battles of Coral Sea and Midway.*

ABOVE: *A* SQUADRON *of Douglas SBD Dauntless are seen over USS* Enterprise *in late 1941, just weeks before the attack on Pearl Harbor. Despite its many shortcomings, the Dauntless played a crucial role in combatting the Japanese in the Pacific, sinking a greater tonnage of shipping than any other Allied aircraft.*

for the strike, shot down 67 Japanese planes. At the same time, American planes were headed directly for Nagumo's carriers. Nagumo still had half of his planes held back in reserve, but he would have to keep his decks clear in order to recover his returning planes, which would be low on fuel. The Japanese strike did not do as much damage to Midway as was needed to ensure an easy invasion. Accordingly, the Japanese attack commander radioed back that another strike against the island was required.

THE CRUCIAL MOMENTS

Meanwhile, the American first strike had reached Nagumo's carriers. It failed, suffering heavy losses, but it revealed to Nagumo the presence of American carriers nearby. Nagumo now faced a dilemma. He had planes out to sea that he

THE SORYU *was designed and laid down in 1937, the first in a new series of fleet carriers that became the mainstay of the Japanese navy during the first years of the war. With an excellent power-to-weight ratio and able to accommodate more than 60 aircraft, the Soryu was fast and agile. However, her light armour made her vulnerable to air attack.*

needed to recover and he had to choose between arming his planes for a second strike on Midway Island or a strike on the American carriers whose exact location was still unknown. The former operation would require high explosive bombs, the latter operation would require torpedoes.

Nagumo first ordered his second wave to be armed with bombs for the second pass at Midway, but at 7.40 a.m. a signal came in from a Japanese cruiser reporting the American carriers east of Nagumo and closing fast. Nagumo thus had the worst possible situation, with enemy carriers nearby, but planes armed with the wrong ordnance for attacking them. He also still had airmen returning to their carrier low on fuel, with several wounded. He ordered his carriers to prepare for recovery of his first strike force, thus losing precious time.

At 9.30 a.m. and 9.40 a.m. two waves of American torpedo bombers attacked the Japanese carriers, but were annihilated by faster, more nimble Japanese fighters. The Americans lost 47 of their 51 planes. The torpedo attacks, although ineffective, kept Nagumo from launching his planes and distracted the Japanese fighters from a more powerful wave of American SBD Dauntless dive bombers. Owing to the good luck that is the result of hard work and good guesswork, the Dauntless bombers had arrived over the Japanese carriers at the perfect time.

Because of the confusion regarding the change of armament, the Japanese carriers had bombs and torpedoes stacked on the decks, instead of safely below in magazines. Because of the need to refuel the returning planes, moreover, the decks were also full of gasoline lines, and the confusion of all this activity prevented Nagumo from being able to launch his reserve fighters.

In this vulnerable position, the Japanese had to face American dive bombers launched from the Yorktown and Enterprise. At 10.22 a.m. American planes struck the *Kaga*, eventually hitting it four times. Within a few short minutes the *Soryu* and *Akagi* had also been hit and put out of action. Fires spread out of control and in at least one case, fire spread to the main ammunition magazines. All three carriers were later abandoned and scuttled. It was an astonishing example of chance meeting skill at just the right moment. In just a few minutes the entire balance of naval power in the Pacific had changed.

FINAL ACTIONS

Aircraft from the lone remaining Japanese carrier, the *Hiryu*, damaged the *Yorktown* badly enough to force Admiral Fletcher to order her to be abandoned. Already in bad shape, she had performed as well as could have been expected, and was later sunk by a Japanese submarine. Later in the day American aircraft spotted the *Hiryu* and scored four direct hits, causing fires that forced her crew to abandon ship. The Japanese had now lost all four of the carriers they had committed to the attack. Total Japanese losses included four carriers, two heavy cruisers, three destroyers, 229 aircraft and 3500 men. American losses included one carrier, one destroyer, 150 aircraft and 307 men.

The Americans knew that they had won a major victory but decided not to risk a night action against the now exposed Japanese surface vessels. They therefore withdrew to the east to the safety of the Midway Island defences, although American cruisers and submarines continued to harass the remaining Japanese ships. The Japanese used the time to withdraw to safety. Yamamoto, for his part, knew how bad the disaster had been for Japan, commenting to his officers, 'I am the only one who must apologize to His Majesty' for the defeat. Yamamoto offered his resignation, but it was declined.

THE LAST SURVIVOR of the Japanese battle fleet at Midway, Hiryu was struck by SBD Dauntless dive bombers late on 4 June 1942. Burning fiercely, the carrier was abandoned and scuttled some 12 hours later.

AFTERMATH

Japanese losses had indeed been severe. In one day they had lost four irreplaceable carriers and as many pilots as their pre-war training system had produced in a year. Japan was left with just two carriers. The Americans had also lost a carrier, but they had an industrial base that eventually produced 35 more carriers by the end of the war. In that same time period, Japan was barely able to make good the losses from Midway alone.

Midway did not, of course, win the Pacific War for the United States. It did, however, shift the strategic initiative to the United States. Without aircraft carriers, the Japanese could not hope to conduct any more long-range surprise operations. As several other events from the war also showed, surface ships, the true strength of the Japanese fleet, were vulnerable without air cover. Future Pacific naval battles bore this dictum out, as Japanese battleships could not operate with impunity as long as American carriers were nearby. Pre-war American faith in the aircraft carrier had been proven justified and as American industry produced more carriers and more planes, the scales tipped increasingly in America's favour.

MIDWAY

NAGUMO – FIRST
CARRIER STRIKE FORCE

HIRYU

KAGA

AKAGI

SORYU

6 *Soryu* is abandoned at 7.10 p.m., while *Kaga* and *Akagi* are scuttled the next day. The bulk of the Japanese carrier fleet has been destroyed in a battle that decisively turns the war in the Pacific in the Allies' favour.

1 At 4.30 a.m. on the 4 June, Admiral Nagumo launches a first wave of 72 bombers and 36 fighters against Midway Island. His fleet was 380km (240 miles) from the target and closing fast.

5 High-level bombing from Douglas Dauntlesses from *Enterprise* and *Yorktown* cause heavy damage to *Soryu, Agaki* and *Kaga*.

KEY
◀ U.S. NAVY
◁ IMPERIAL JAPANESE NAVY
✕✕ U.S. AIRCRAFT
✕✕ JAPANESE AIRCRAFT

FLETCHER (TF17)

SPRUANCE (TF16)

USS YORKTOWN

USS ENTERPRISE

USS HORNET

4 Unbeknown to Nagumo, the US carrier fleet is closing fast. At 8.00 a.m. a 151-aircraft strike is launched against the Japanese fleet, while they are recovering and rearming their aircraft from the first strike against Midway.

3 On Midway, between 7.05 a.m. and 8.10 a.m., all the base's offensive aircraft are sent to intercept the Japanese fleet in three waves. Although attacking bravely, the US airplanes have little impact. However, Nagumo decides a second attack on the Midway is necessary to immobilize the airstrip and neutralize the US aircraft there.

2 At 6.16 a.m., the radar station on Midway detects the incoming Japanese aircraft and US aircraft are scrambled to intercept. However, the slow Grumman Wildcats and Brewster Buffulos are no match for the superior Zeros.

MIDWAY ISLAND

NORMANDY 1944

The battle for Normandy began with the spectacularly successful D-Day landings, thanks in no small part to an astounding deception campaign which mislead the German commanders completely. However, the breakout from Normandy was more problematic, and was only achieved after hard and costly fighting.

O n the USA's entry into the World War II in December 1941, the Americans and their British allies agreed on a policy of defeating Germany first, while containing the Japanese in the Pacific. It was clear that the defeat of Nazi Germany would eventually entail the landing of an Allied army on the European mainland. The British and Americans differed in how this should be achieved.

For the Americans the issue was simple, a large force should be landed in northwest Europe to defeat the bulk of German forces and then march on Berlin. British military leaders, haunted by the slaughter of the World War I and having experienced German military prowess, were less enthusiastic. They preferred a

NORMANDY FACTS

Who: American, British, Canadian and French forces under the supreme command of General Dwight D. Eisenhower (1890–1969) against the German armies in the West commanded by Field Marshal Gerd von Rundstedt (1875–1953).

What: After the largest amphibious landings in military history, the Allies were able to establish themselves on the Continent and break out of Normandy after harder-than-expected fighting.

Where: The Normandy peninsula in western France.

When: 6 June – 19 August 1944.

Why: The Allies sought to establish a Second Front, liberate Western Europe and drive on into Nazi Germany.

Outcome: The German Army in Normandy was effectively destroyed and the Allies advanced east towards the German border.

AMERICAN INFANTRY WADE ASHORE on Omaha Beach. These are almost certainly part of a later wave of troops to land, since they are not encoutering the deathly fire experienced by the earlier waves. Despite the low-lying cloud apparent in this photograph, the weather cleared in the afternoon, allowing Allied airpower to dominate the battlefield.

strategy of dispersing German strength by continuing the campaign in the Mediterranean. For a while the British policy prevailed, but at the Casablanca Conference of January 1943, the British were forced to accept American military logic and agree to a major military landing in France. In May a provisional date for the operation, now code-named 'Overlord', was set for 1 May 1944.

OPERATION 'OVERLORD'

The prospect of transporting enough troops across the English Channel to establish and hold a beachhead and then reinforcing them faster than the Germans could bolster their own forces was a daunting task. Eschewing the most direct route across the Straits of Dover, the planners decided to land in Normandy. This was largely because it was within the range of Allied air cover, had firm and sheltered beaches and was close to a major port, Cherbourg. General Dwight D. Eisenhower was appointed Supreme Commander with General Bernard Montgomery (1887–1976) as the commander of the invasion's land forces. They immediately

RIGHT: GENERAL EISENHOWER gives a pep talk to members of the 101st Airborne prior to their drop on the Normandy countryside.

BELOW: A BRITISH SERGEANT SMILES for the camera as infantry form up on Sword Beach, ready to support the armour that is preparing to move off. The men have canvas covers for the bolts of their rifles, to protect them from the sea water and sand as they landed.

altered the original plan, by widening the beachhead and expanding the initial amphibious assault from three divisions to five, supported by various commando and Ranger units, with three airborne divisions dropped inland to secure the flanks. They would be rapidly followed by the rest of the US First Army under General Omar Bradley (1893–1981) and the British Second Army commanded by General Sir Miles Dempsey (1896–1969). By late 1943, it was clear to the Germans that an Anglo-American invasion would come; it was just a question of when and where. Most of the German commanders, Hitler included, believed that the Allies would attempt to land on the Pas de Calais. Field Marshal von Rundstedt, the German Commander-in-Chief in the West, had 58 divisions under his command, but half of these were static, tied to stretches of coastal defences. Key to the defeat of any Allied invasion, was his nine panzer and one panzergrenadier divisions. However, he disagreed with his subordinate Field Marshal Erwin Rommel (1891–1944), commander of Army Group B, made up of Fifteenth Army in the Pas de Calais and Seventh Army protecting Normandy, as to how that armour should be used.

Von Rundstedt and General von Schweppenburg, commander of Panzer Group West, wanted the armour held back to deliver a crushing counter-attack. Rommel felt this would be impossible given Allied control of the air. He believed that the Germans had to defeat the invasion on the beaches and thus he wanted the armour deployed as close to the beaches as possible. Hitler's solution was a compromise. In Normandy this meant only one panzer division, the 21st, was located close to the coast with the rest, Panzer Lehr and 12th SS Panzer, held further back. This left both commanders dissatisfied; Rommel felt his forward defences were inadequate and Von Rundstedt believed his panzer reserve was too small.

DECEPTION PLANS

For 'Overlord' to succeed, the Allies had to train and then assemble their forces in southern England. The Air Commander-in-Chief, Air Chief Marshal Leigh-Mallory (1892–1944) had to ensure air superiority over the beaches and hamper German supply and reinforcement capabilities. The Allied air forces targeted the French transport system, but in such a way so as not to draw attention to Normandy. An intricate deception plan, Operation 'Fortitude' sought to convince the Germans that, firstly, the Pas de Calais was the intended target and, secondly, the actual invasion of Normandy was simply a diversion. This succeeded perfectly.

The Allies assembled a vast invasion fleet of nearly 7000 warships, transports and support vessels to escort and provide fire support or carry the 130,000 troops across the Channel. During 5 June, after a 24-hour delay due to bad weather, the fleet assembled off the south coast of England and began to sail south towards the six landing beaches in Normandy, designated from west to east, 'Utah', 'Omaha', 'Gold', 'Juno' and 'Sword'. They were passed overhead by the first Allied bombers

JUST 12.5M (41ft) in length, the LCA (landing craft assault) were some of the smaller craft used to transport troops on D-Day, carrying about 30 personnel.

SHERMAN D-D TANK

The DD (Duplex Drive) Sherman was amphibious version of the mainstay of main Anglo-American tank. A collapsible fabric screen and inflatable pillars and two small propellers allowed the tank to 'swim'. Once it was ashore, the screen could be collapsed and the DD Sherman could function as a normal tank.

en route to attack the German defences. These were followed from 11.30 p.m. by the transport planes taking the 17,000 airborne troops to drop zones to the east and west of the beaches.

D-DAY

The Battle of Normandy opened just after midnight on 6 June as the British 6th Airborne Division landed north-east of Caen. The first troops into action were glider-borne troops of 2nd Oxford and Buckinghamshire Light Infantry who quickly secured the bridges over the Caen canal and the River Orne. Other units of the 6th Airborne captured several bridges over the Orne, overran the Melville Battery and secured the invasion's left flank by holding the Ranville-Hérouvillette area. Meanwhile at about 1.00 a.m. the American paratroops of the 82nd and 101st Airborne

Divisions jumped into the marshy terrain around the westernmost landing beach 'Utah'. The paratroopers did much to confuse the German response, which was not helped by the fact that Rommel was on leave. 'Fortitude' had also ensured that the Germans continued to expect the main invasion in the Pas de Calais even several days after D-Day and thus held back their reserves.

Two hours later 1900 bombers began attacking the German defences in the landing area and as dawn approached the naval bombardment opened. At 6.30 a.m. the Americans of 4th Division began their run-in at 'Utah' beach; the Canadians attacking 'Juno' beach would land as late as 7.45 a.m. as a result of tidal conditions. On 'Utah' the Americans quickly established themselves ashore, advanced across the waterlogged terrain behind the beach and linked up with airborne forces in the area. This was achieved for the cost of just under 200 casualties.

Things went rather less well on 'Omaha' beach. Allied intelligence had failed notice that the defending regiment of the 716th Division, a static formation, had been reinforced by two regiments of the veteran 352nd Division. These men largely survived the preparatory bombardment unscathed. On top of this the poor weather conditions meant that only five of the 32 DD swimming Sherman tanks and very few of the Americans' supporting combat engineers made it ashore. The assaulting troops of 1st Infantry and 29th National Guard Divisions took terrible losses to the well dug-in German troops. By the end of the day they had secured a tenuous foothold no deeper than 1.8km (2000 yards) at the cost of 2000 casualties.

'Gold' was the westernmost Anglo-Canadian beach. It was assaulted by the British 50th (Northumbrian) Division. Unlike the Americans, the British were

THIS US INFANTRY CAPTAIN *carries an M1 Carbine. The carbine was designed for specialist troops such as drivers and machine gunners, but such was its lightness and ease of handling it became popular with front-line troops.*

supported by a variety of specialized armoured fighting vehicles, such as AVRE assault tanks, to breach defences and Sherman Crab flail tanks, designed to clear minefields, in addition to their DD tanks. By the end of the day, 50th Division had managed to push 6.4km (4 miles) inland while 47 Commando struck westwards towards the Americans on Omaha.

Meanwhile the 3rd Canadian Infantry Division landed on 'Juno', the central British-Canadian beach. They met particularly strong resistance and were hampered by the loss of many landing craft to submerged obstacles. It took the Canadians an hour and a quarter of hard fighting to secure the first exits from the beach. They also managed to push about 6.4km (4 miles) inland by the end of the day.

On 'Sword' the most easterly beach, effective fire support suppressed the enemy defences and most the landing craft taking ashore the 3rd Infantry Division made the run-in undamaged. However, due to the bad weather the incoming tide was higher than expected, which meant the craft were deposited amongst the German submerged beach obstacles that the Allies had expected to be visible. Landing higher up the beach than expected did have the advantage of reducing the amount of ground the infantry had to cross, but in confined space of the beach armoured vehicles soon became congested, hampering the British attempt to push inland. The 3rd Division was tasked with linking up with 6th Airborne on the River Orne, which 1st Special Service Brigade and 8th Brigade achieved reasonably quickly. However, the capture of Caen, which was also scheduled for the first day, proved a little more difficult. The drive on the city was disrupted by a counter-attack by 21st Panzer. The German division drove straight into the gap between 'Juno' and 'Sword' beaches, but faltered in the face of British anti-tank and tank gunnery.

THE BATTLE FOR CAEN

Caen had not fallen, but otherwise it had been a remarkably successful day. The Allies had achieved massive strategic surprise and landed over 130,000 men at the cost of about 6000 US and 4300 British and Canadian casualties. The Germans had failed to drive them back into the sea and over the next few days the beachheads were linked up and resources poured into the Normandy pocket. By D-Day +6 about 330,000 men, 55,000 vehicles and 104,000 tons of supplies had been landed.

However, a rapid break-out did not follow. The Americans pushed up into the Cotentin Peninsula towards Cherbourg, while British and Canadians concentrated on the capture of Caen. Montgomery's plan for Normandy was for the British to tie down the weight of German resources, particularly their armour, to give the Americans the opportunity to break-out in the face of weaker resistance.

LIKE THIS MACHINE-GUN EMPLACEMENT, some of the defences on the Atlantic Wall had been taken from the French Maginot Line and other obstacles built by the Belgians and Dutch in the late 1930s. Many of these old defences proved very effective against the advancing Allies.

Army Group. Lack of resistance in Brittany allowed Patton to shift the bulk of his forces westwards. Despite the imminent collapse of the German position, Hitler insisted on a counter-offensive, which was launched against the US First Army in the Mortain area on 7 August, but the Germans only succeeded in pushing their remaining armour further westwards into a pocket that was rapidly closing around them. This gave Bradley the idea of pushing Patton's troops at Le Mans northwards, while the Canadians drove south towards Falaise, a move that might trap an estimated 21 German divisions in the pocket. Montgomery immediately approved and although the two armies did not meet until 19 August, some 10,000 Germans were killed and 50,000 captured. About 20,000 escaped. The battle for Normandy was over.

AFTERMATH

The Normandy Landings were an extraordinary achievement, easily the largest amphibious operation in history. The Allies had managed to establish themselves on a hostile coastline and reinforce their position faster than their enemy, who relied on the comprehensive road and rail network of northwestern Europe. Much of the success was down to an impressive logistical effort by the Allies and the importance of air power in hampering the German response. The landings did not lead to a rapid break-out and collapse of the German position in the west, but the Normandy Campaign caused losses to the Germans in terms of men and material and the establishment, at last, of the Second Front meant that Germany's strategic position was now untenable.

AN MG42 MACHINE GUNNER, of the Waffen-SS 'Hitler Jugend' Division. This division was brought in as reinforcements to stem the Allied advance.

This was a reasonable enough strategy but his reputation with his allies and posterity was not well served by his overconfident predictions of success for the operations to capture Caen. A Canadian push on the city on 7 June floundered in the face on the arrival of 12th SS Panzer Division, a broad outflanking manoeuvre was stopped at Villers-Bocage on 12 June and the carefully prepared Operation 'Epsom' from 25–30 June failed in the face of desperate German counter-attacks. The city finally fell on 8 July. Even then the British failed to break-out towards Falaise and took massive losses, particularly in tanks, during Operation 'Goodwood' from 18–20 July.

THE BREAKOUT

Nonetheless these operations had had the desired effect of sucking the German armoured forces into a battle of attrition on the western side of the lodgement. The German commanders had hoped to husband their panzer divisions for a counter-attack that would drive the Allies into the sea, but had been forced to fritter these resources away in a desperate attempt to shore up the line in the face of constant British pressure. Meanwhile the Americans had managed to capture Cherbourg and as 'Goodwood' drew in the bulk of German armour in Normandy, they prepared an offensive to capitalize on the weakened German line in front of them. This would be the crowning achievement of the campaign. On the morning of 25 July a massive air bombardment heralded the opening of Operation 'Cobra'. American infantry and armour broke through the German lines and headed south for Coutances. After two days fighting it was clear that the Americans had destroyed the Germans' left flank and opened up the way into Brittany. On 1 August, the US Third Army under General George Patton (1885–1945) became operational and Bradley handed 1st Army over to General Hodges, stepping up to take command of Twelfth

NORMANDY

FALAISE

5 21st Panzer Division, the only armoured division in the vicinity, counter-attacked and although halted, disrupted the British drive towards Caen.

1 Just after midnight British airborne troops land, seizing bridges across the Orne and Caen Canal, overrunning the Merville Battery and securing the invasion's left flank.

CAEN

352

716

SWORD

JUNO

GOLD

BRITISH 6 AIRBORNE
AND GLIDER TROOPS

4 Between 6.30 a.m and 7.45 a.m. the run-in of the five spearhead divisions and supporting special forces began. By the end of the day all five were established ashore.

CRERAR
I CORPS

DEMPSEY
2 ARMY

3 At 3.00 a.m., 1900 Allied bombers attacked the German defences in the landing area followed by a naval bombardment from seven battleships, 18 cruisers, 43 destroyers and a monitor.

91 · COUTANCE

2 At 1.00 a.m. US airborne troops landed to the west of Utah beach to secure the western flank of the invasion beaches.

ST LÔ

109

CARENTAN

BAYEUX

243

OMAHA

UTAH

US 82 AND 101 AIRBORNE

COLLINS VII CORPS

BUCKNALL XXX CORPS

GEROW V CORPS

BRADLEY 1 ARMY

KEY

◀ ALLIED FORCES

✕ ALLIED DIVISION

▬ ALLIED ARMOUR

◀ GERMAN FORCES

✕ GERMAN DIVISION

THE TET OFFENSIVE
1968

As 1967 drew to a close, it appeared that the United States was gaining the upper hand in the Vietnam War. The Tet Offensive of early 1968, however, began the steady decline of US fortunes in Vietnam, despite an undeniable military victory.

From 1965 to the end of 1967, the principal US strategy in Vietnam was 'search and destroy' (S&D), an attritional form of warfare developed by General William Westmoreland (1914–2005), head of the Military Assistance Command, Vietnam (MACV), and other high-ranking US staff. S&D tactics concentrated on stacking up high body counts of North Vietnamese Army (NVA) and Viet Cong (VC) personnel, utilizing the massive US advantage in firepower and manoeuvre formations. The aim was to reach the 'crossover point', where North Vietnam was simply unable to prosecute the war militarily owing to manpower losses.

THE TET OFFENSIVE FACTS

Who: The regular forces of the North Vietnamese Army (NVA) supported by the irregular Viet Cong (VC), numbering around 80,000. They took on the full might of the US forces in Vietnam, plus the Army of the Republic of South Vietnam (ARVN), a combined force of over 1.5 million.

What: Communist forces launch a major offensive throughout South Vietnam, targeting urban areas and military bases.

Where: The Tet Offensive was launched along the entire length and breadth of South Vietnam, from military bases along the Demilitarized Zone (DMZ) in the north, down to the Mekong Delta in the south.

When: 29 January–8 April 1968.

Why: The North Vietnamese hoped to occupy South Vietnam's urban centres and draw out a popular uprising against the South Vietnamese government.

Outcome: Total military defeat for the NVA and VC, although the Western media focus more on the seeming escalation of the conflict rather than US successes.

US M113 ARMOURED PERSONNEL CARRIERS (APCs) advance into Saigon to combat the Viet Cong uprising. The US use of heavy firepower in urban zones, particularly of artillery and air assets, would cause great controversy in the media.

TET OFFENSIVE – HUE

1 On 31 January combined NVA and VC forces launch a rocket and mortar attack on ARVN units in the north and west of the city. AVRN forces are driven back.

OLD CITY

IMPERIAL PALACE

4 On 12 February, the 1st Batallion US Marines is deployed to the Old City by landing craft and helicopter to break the stalemate there. Bitter house-to-house fighting continues for two more weeks.

PERFUME RIVER

KEY

US MARINES

COMMUNIST FORCES

5 On 24 February the final attacks are launched and US and AVRN forces finally gain control of Hue.

2 A US Marine force sent to assist crosses the Perfume River but is forced to fall back amidst determined communist attacks.

3 On 1 February AVRN forces begin counter-attacking in the Old City while the US Marines begin clearing the New City. By 9 February, US forces control the New City south of the river.

NEW CITY

OPERATION 'IRAQI FREEDOM'
2003

Operation 'Iraqi Freedom' was boldly conceived and vigorously executed. In less than 40 days US-led Coalition forces crushed Iraqi military resistance, captured Baghdad and removed the regime of Saddam Hussein.

The traumatic events in Iraq following the completion of Operation 'Iraqi Freedom' have tended to cloud judgement about the sheer success of the initial military operation. 'Iraqi Freedom' was arguably one of the best-executed military campaigns of the last 60 years, an action in which the domination of Coalition forces was total and their casualties incredibly light. This is not to deny that there were problems in both game plan and execution, but such are the stuff of war, and the aggregate operation was a resounding triumph.

OPERATION 'IRAQI FREEDOM' FACTS

Who: A US-led Coalition force of over 260,000 troops against the national defence forces of Iraq and Fedayeen irregulars.

What: The full-scale invasion of Iraq by the Coalition, with its objective as the destruction of Iraqi forces and the overthrow of Saddam Hussein's regime.

Where: The main theatre of the conflict was concentrated between the Iraq-Kuwait border and Baghdad, with a separate theatre in the north that was mainly in the hands of US-supported Kurdish separatists.

When: 20 March–1 May 2003.

Why: 'Iraqi Freedom' was part of the US response to the 11 September 2001 terrorist attacks, based on claims that Iraq had broken UN sanctions, sponsored terrorist groups and illegally possessed weapons of mass destruction (WMDs).

Outcome: Successful occupation of Iraq by Coalition forces, although the campaign ended with a dramatic rise in insurgency actions.

US MISSILES *slam into key targets around Baghdad on 21 March 2003. The Iraqi forces generally expected a re-run of the 1990-91 Gulf War, when the Allies pre-empted the land war with a prolonged air campaign. Instead, US and British land units crossed into Iraq almost immediately.*

A REPUBLICAN GUARD soldier. The Republican Guard put up the sternest resistance to Operation Iraqi Freedom, but, suffering from low morale and a poor command structure, they were totally outmanoeuvred and outgunned by US armoured forces.

OPPOSING FORCES

On 17 March 2003, President George W. Bush gave a clear ultimatum to the Iraqi leadership: 'Saddam Hussein and his sons must leave Iraq within 48 hours. Their refusal to go will result in military conflict commenced at a time of our choosing.' His threat was backed by the presence of over 260,000 Coalition troops (214,000 US and 45,000 British, the rest being small contingents from allied nations) massed in border staging areas in Kuwait. Facing them was uncertainty. Iraq's military forces had certainly been degraded by the destruction of the 1990–1 Gulf War and the subsequent

military sanctions against the country, and both morale and command initiative were poor. Yet intelligence estimates placed the number of available regular troops at over 400,000 (including 44,000 Fedayeen Saddam paramilitaries) with up to 650,000 reserves. Even allowing for inadequacies in combat capability, that still amounted to a potent force, especially if it had taken on board combat lessons learnt in the first Gulf War.

The Iraqi military, however, was expecting a re-run of the earlier conflict – with its extended air campaign prologue. They would soon be disabused. Under the overall leadership of General Tommy Franks (Commander-in-Chief, US Central Command), the Coalition forces would launch an immediate land campaign, securing key positions in southern Iraq while other units drove northwards to the capital Baghdad. The aim was to bypass many of Iraq's major urban centres (there was the concern that the Iraqi army would opt for urban battlefields to avoid their technological disadvantages in open terrain warfare), pushing straight through to Baghdad and enforcing rapid regime change by crushing the top of the command structure. With no response to Bush's ultimatum, Operation 'Iraqi Freedom' began on 19 March.

SOUTHERN ACTIONS

The first actions of 'Iraqi Freedom' were, as in 1991, an air attack. US attack aircraft and Tomahawk cruise missiles made precision strikes against targets across Baghdad, hoping to take out Saddam Hussein and 55 key Iraqi leaders (this 'decapitation' strike was largely unsuccessful). Shortly after, on the night

LEFT: THE US M1A1 ABRAMS tank often formed the vanguard of the US push up towards Baghdad. Its Rheinmetall 120mm (4.724in) smoothbore gun can hit targets at well over visual range with either depleted uranium or high-explosive anti-tank (HEAT) rounds.

THE T-55 was one of the oldest tanks in the Iraqi arsenal by 2003. Although some models had received upgrade packages to armour, fire-control systems and main armament, they were still hopelessly outclassed by the US and British tanks.

A UH-60 BLACKHAWK helicopter flies over Baghdad in May 2003. Although helicopters were ideally suited to operations over the Iraqi wilderness, they proved very vulnerable to opportunistic small-arms fire over urban zones.

of the 20th/21st, Coalition forces surged across the Iraq-Kuwait border. The attack plan for the south (operations in northern Iraq are considered in the feature box) was three-pronged. The US Army V Corps, led by the 3rd Infantry Division, would drive up towards Baghdad through the desert on the western side of the Euphrates River. East of the river, the 1st Marine Expeditionary Force (MEF) would push through An Nasiriyah, cross the Euphrates, and advance on Baghdad from east of the river, thereby forming one arm of a pincer movement with the army formations. Finally, British forces, with US Marine support, would operate in the far south of the country, securing the Al Faw peninsula and taking Iraq's second city, Basra.

Operation 'Iraqi Freedom' got off to a brisk start. Iraqi border outposts were obliterated by artillery fire and precision attacks from US Army Apache helicopters, allowing easy movement into Iraq. Late on 20 March, British and US Marines stormed and secured the port of Umm Qasr (although sporadic combat would continue for the next two days), before the US elements turned northwards. The Al Faw peninsula was occupied by a combined arms amphibious operation, and by 21 March the British 7th Armoured Brigade had reached the outskirts of Basra. Resistance

toughened here against Iraqi militia and regular forces. Fearing a horrific civilian casualty toll in an urban battle, the British stopped and waited, allowing Basra's civilians free passage out of the city. Events in southern Iraq were unfolding rapidly. The 1st Marine Division secured the Rumaila oilfields in the south of Iraq – one of the world's largest petroleum/gas reserves – before turning west towards An Nasiriyah. The task of actually securing An Nasiriyah, with its vital series of bridges over the Euphrates, fell to Task Force Tarawa, otherwise known as the 2nd Marine Expeditionary Brigade (MEB). There it would experience one of the campaign's nastier shocks.

AN NASIRIYAH AND BEYOND

The greatest challenges for the Coalition assault into Iraq were time and distance. With every hour of advance the Allied supply lines became increasingly stretched. By the end of 22 March, for example, the 3rd Infantry Division was 241km (150 miles) into Iraq. This supply line had to be protected, and there remained the worrying possibility that the advance might slow down to a stop, and allow the Iraqi forces to cut up an over-extended Coalition. Yet although resistance was locally fierce, so far it was not heavy enough to affect overall strategy. Iraq troops seemed more inclined to surrender than die in a hail of US gunfire.

However, on 23 March events took a worrying turn around An Nasiriyah. A US Army unit, the 507th Maintenance Company (part of the 3rd Infantry Division, which was also participating in actions around An Nasiriyah) was ambushed by Fedayeen fighters, who killed 11 soldiers and took seven prisoner (including the now famous Private Jessica Lynch). Marines of Task Force Tarawa moved to the rescue, but the day descended into a bloody

OPERATIONS IN NORTHERN IRAQ

The original plan for Operation 'Iraqi Freedom' had involved a matching offensive down into northern Iraq from Turkey. However, the Turkish government prohibited Turkey's use as a jumping-off point for US land forces (it permitted the use of air bases), so the action in the north was mainly concentrated in the hands of Kurdish Peshmerga paramilitaries acting with strong support from the US 10th Special Forces Group. Furthermore, a 1000-soldier airdrop from the 173rd Airborne Brigade secured Bashur airfield, and gave the Kurds more conventional power. Iraqi troops in the north began to retreat southwards, and on 28 March US and Kurdish troops took the base camp of Ansar al-Islam, an Islamic group connected with the al-Qaeda terrorist organization, after a particular violent battle code-named Operation 'Viking'. In a subsequent action known as the Battle of the Green Line, another Kurdish/US force (operating, as usual, with good close-air support) defeated the Iraqi 13th Infantry Division, and then occupied Tikrit, securing Saddam Hussein's last possible bastion of resistance.

battle in what would become known as 'ambush alley'. Eighteen Marines were killed, several by the 'friendly fire' of supporting A10 aircraft. It would take until the end of the month to secure An Nasiriyah, although by then the Marine advance northwards had resumed. The three Regimental Combat Teams (RCTs) of 1st MEF took two lines of advance towards Baghdad: 5th RCT and 7th RCT took Route 1 directly towards the capital, while 1st RCT swung up Route 7 further east.

The US advance was becoming tougher. Out to the west, the main US Army advance was facing increasing resistance from four Republican Guard divisions, and by 25 March the 3rd Infantry Division was locked in combat around An Najaf (over 300 Iraqi troops were killed in just two days of fighting). Furthermore, a huge sandstorm across the region had reduced the Coalition advance to a grinding crawl,

A BRITISH SNIPER serving with the 1st Battalion, Irish Guards, takes up a position close to the city of Basra, April 2003. Snipers were set up to provide protection for British Army engineers employed to put out the numerous oil-well fires started by retreating Iraqi forces.

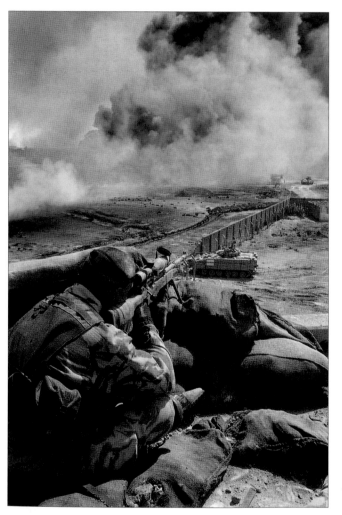

giving Iraqi irregulars a breathing space in which to redeploy and attack the supply lines.

An Najaf was steadily brought under control by US forces: encircled on 26 March, hammered with artillery and air bombardment, then finally stormed and controlled at the beginning of April by the 101st Airborne Division. By this point, however, the Coalition was closing on the capital.

BATTLE FOR BAGHDAD

In the far south of Iraq, battle was still raging for Basra. A large tank battle around the city on 27 March saw the Royal Scots Dragoon Guards destroy 14 Iraqi tanks. On 30 March, Operation 'James', a major offensive into the city, was launched by the 7th Armoured Brigade, supported by the Parachute Regiment and Special Forces soldiers. Hard fighting continued for a week, but by 6 April the city was finally in British hands. However, the sudden collapse of the city's administration led to an anarchic upsurge in looting and random violence, a story that would become familiar across Iraq over the coming weeks.

While the British were fighting for Basra, the US 3rd Infantry Division assaulted around the western side of Karbala, crossed the Euphrates, and closed on Baghdad. By now the resistance from Iraqi Army forces was collapsing. The Republican Guard's Medina Division on the Baghdad outskirts, for example, was obliterated on 3–4 April, as was a Fedayeen counter-attack. To the east, the Marines were also closing up on the city.

The US commanders decided on a bold strategy to take Baghdad. On 5 April, the heavily armed 2nd Brigade, 3rd Infantry, made a 'thunder run' up Route 8 straight into the capital. The unit consisted of 761 men backed by tanks and Bradley armoured fighting vehicles, and was essentially a reconnaissance force to test out the Baghdad resistance. Under heavy fire all the way (every vehicle was hit), the unit then swung out to reach the Saddam International Airport, already in US hands.

On 7 April, a second 'thunder run' was made, this time plunging into the administrative heart of the capital. By nightfall Saddam's palaces were in US hands, but fighting to secure the supply route was fierce, with constant firefights along the snaking streets. US Marine units were now entering and securing eastern parts of the city, having forced their way across the Diyala Bridge. By 8 April the Marines had closed up to the Tigris River, effectively completing the occupation of the city. On 9 April, in a highly symbolic moment, the towering statue of Saddam Hussein in Firdos Square was pulled down by an American armoured vehicle.

The formal land campaign to take Iraq was effectively over. Saddam Hussein's home town of Tikrit was captured by a US Marine task force on 15 April, removing the last significant outpost of resistance in central Iraq, and by 10

AN F/A-18 HORNET from the 'Silver Eagles' of Marine Fighter Attack Squadron One Fifteen (VMFA-115) launches from the flight deck of USS Harry S. Truman in support of Operation 'Iraqi Freedom'. Coalition air superiority was essential in guaranteeing a quick victory in Iraq.

April the campaign in the north had secured Kirkuk. On 1 May 2003, President Bush landed on the flight deck of the USS *Abraham Lincoln* and declared an official end to the combat operations in Iraq.

AFTERMATH

History now shows us that President Bush's dramatic declaration of the end of hostilities was deeply flawed. Poor post-operation planning fanned the flames of a spiralling insurgency in Iraq which, at the time of writing, accounts for several thousand lives in Baghdad alone every month. One of the salient features of Operation 'Iraqi Freedom' was that large sections of the Iraqi public were alienated by Coalition military action.

Around 30,000 Iraqi civilians were killed during the operation, and evidence suggests that a high percentage of these was caused by indiscriminate US firepower rather than enemy actions. Furthermore, the fall of Saddam's regime and the inadvisable disbandment of the Iraqi army fuelled an explosion of inter-tribal and inter-faith conflicts, leading to a dreadful existence for many Iraqi people.

'Iraqi Freedom' itself was not without faults. Many commanders on the ground felt that Defense Secretary

A SQUAD OF US ARMY SOLDIERS from the 23rd Infantry Regiment conduct an area reconnaissance mission in Baghdad, August 2006. More than three years after hostilities were declared, large numbers of Coalition troops were bogged down in anti-insurgency warfare.

Donald Rumsfeld's decision to limit troop numbers caused severe problems for the advance and security actions, and actions at An Nasiriyah and other places showed how effective a determined insurgency force could be. Yet war is at heart a violent, problematic encounter, and judged by the light casualties – less than 130 US personnel and 33 British personnel killed – and the swiftness with which the objectives were achieved, it is an impressive model of a modern land campaign.

OPERATION 'IRAQI FREEDOM'

MOSUL

SYRIA

TIKRIT

AL-RUTBAH

3 US 3rd Infantry Division forces encircle An Najaf on 26 March, and move up to assault Karbala in preparation for the drive against Baghdad itself, while Marine units swing in from the east.

KEY

Coalition Forces

U.S. Airborne

British Armour

U.S. Armour

Iraqi Armour

Iraqi Army bases

Iraqi Air Force bases

SAUDI ARABIA

5 US Special Forces and airborne units in the northern theatre support Kurdish fighters, who secure Kirkuk on 10 April. A US Marine team takes Tikrit, Saddam Hussein's home town, on 15 April.

KIRKUK

IRAN

4 Following two armoured 'thunder runs' into Baghdad by US forces, the capital city is occupied by 9 April, completing the Allies' regime change objective.

BAGHDAD

2 US Marine and Army forces cross the Euphrates at An Nasiriyah, despite constant attacks, and form the eastern pincer of the drive towards Baghdad.

KUT

KARBALA

AN NAJAF

AN NASIRIYAH

BASRA

1 On 20/21 March Coalition ground forces launch the land campaign into Iraq from cross-border positions in Kuwait. The initial assault consists of a US drive northwards parallel to the Euphrates, and a mainly British swing east through Uum Qasr and towards Basra.

US 1ST MARINE EXP. FORCE

UMM QASR

KUWAIT

US 3RD INF DIV

UK 7TH ARMOURED BDE

INDEX

Page numbers in *italics* refer to illustrations; those in **bold** type refer to map illustrations with text. Abbreviations are as follows: (B) – battle; (NB) – naval battle; (S) – siege.